ALSO BY DAVID KUSHNER

The World's Most Dangerous Geek: And Other True Hacking Stories

Prepare to Meet Thy Doom: And More True Gaming Stories

The Bones of Marianna: A Reform School, a Terrible Secret, and a Hundred-Year Fight for Justice

Jacked: The Outlaw Story of Grand Theft Auto

Levittown: Two Families, One Tycoon, and the Fight for Civil Rights in America's Legendary Suburb

Jonny Magic and the Card Shark Kids: How a Gang of Geeks Beat the Odds and Stormed Las Vegas

Masters of Doom: How Two Guys Created an Empire and Transformed Pop Culture

Alligator Candy

A Memoir

DAVID KUSHNER

SIMON & SCHUSTER

New York London Toronto Sydney New Delhi

Simon & Schuster
1230 Avenue of the Americas
New York, NY 10020

First Simon & Schuster hardcover edition March 2016

Manufactured in the United States of America

3 5 7 9 10 8 6 4 2

Library of Congress Cataloging-in-Publication Data
Kushner, David, 1968– author.
Alligator candy : a memoir / by David Kushner.
pages cm
1. Kushner, Jonathan Mark, 1962–1973. 2. Murder victims—Florida—Tampa—Biography. 3. Murder victims' families—Florida—Tampa—Biography. 4. Children of anthropologists—Biography. 5. Kushner, David, 1968– I. Title.
HV6534.T36K87 2016
362.88—dc23
2015022792

ISBN 978-1-4516-8253-3
ISBN 978-1-4516-8263-2 (ebook)

For Jonathan Kushner

I shall tell you everything, my son. You have the right to know. And besides, you are aware of it all. Where you are, only truth matters, nothing else exists.

—Elie Wiesel, *The Fifth Son*

Part I

1

MY LAST MEMORY of my brother Jon was my most suspect. It was October 28, 1973, and we were on the sidewalk outside our house. I was a stocky four-year-old with a brown bowl haircut, and Jon, wiry and lean with wavy red hair, was eleven. Earlier that year, we'd moved to this small ranch house with a red Spanish-style roof in Tampa, Florida. It was the northern edge of the burgeoning suburbs, a new home on the newest street by the woods. For the kids in the neighborhood, the woods represented the great unknown, a thicket of freedom, a mossy maze of cypress and palms begging to be explored. Kids ventured into there on horseback, barefoot, on bikes. They had worn a path to the 7-Eleven convenience store across the woods, and that's where Jon was heading this day.

Jon straddled his red bicycle, aiming for the trees. These were the *Easy Rider* years, and boys' bikes were designed to resemble motorcycles, the kinds we'd see driven around town by Hells Angels. Jon's bike had a long red banana-shaped seat, shiny chrome upright handlebars, and fat tires. For added effect, kids would tape a playing card in the back spokes to sound like a motorcycle when the tire spun. They'd lower their heads, extend their arms, and hunch their backs as they pedaled, visions of Evel Knievel in their minds.

My parents had given Jon a green ten-speed Schwinn for his birthday in September, but for some reason he decided to ride his old one this morning. Maybe he wanted something more rugged for the woods or just wanted to take one more spin on his old bike before retiring it. He wore a brown muscle shirt and cutoff blue jean shorts embroidered with a patch from his day camp, Camp Keystone. His sneakers were red, white, and blue Hush Puppies. I could tell by the way his feet bobbed on the pedals that he was anxious to leave.

"You're going to forget," I told him.

"I'm not," he replied.

"I know you are."

"I won't."

"Let me go with you."

"You can't. You're too young."

I wanted something specific from the store: Snappy Gator Gum. It wasn't just gum, it was a toy. The gum came packed in the mouth of a plastic alligator head that opened and closed when you squeezed the neck. I had to have it and didn't want anything to get in the way.

"What if it rains?" I asked Jon. I was thinking about an afternoon at our last house, when Jon had biked to a store shortly before a torrential Florida downpour. I remembered standing next to my mom in the kitchen when Jon called, and my mom telling me that we had to go pick him up in the station wagon because he was, as she said, "caught in the rain." I hadn't heard that phrase before, and it struck me as strange. I pictured Jon literally caught in the rain, stuck in suspended animation, hovering in a cage of falling drops.

"If it rains I'll call," he promised.

"Call me anyway when you get there," I said, "so I can remind you what I want."

"Fine."

Jon grabbed the handlebars and pedaled quickly down the sidewalk toward the woods. I watched him ride off, still wishing I could go along. I never saw him again. It would take decades to unravel what happened. But my search would always lead me back to this spot.

2

LIKE MOST parents at the time, my father and mother, Gilbert and Lorraine, didn't worry about Jon riding off into the woods alone. They were raising their children—Jon and me and our thirteen-year-old brother Andy—in a different age and a different spirit than the one in which I'm now raising my own.

It was the early seventies. The Age of Aquarius had given way to the "Free to Be You and Me" generation. We were unbuckled and unrestrained, free from seat belts or helmets or meticulously organized playdates. Our parents let us climb over the seats of our smoke-filled station wagon, puffing on candy cigarettes and, on road trips, sleeping way in the back. When we had a stretch of hours to play, they let us put the free in free time, wandering off to learn and explore and find adventures. They shared our innocence. They hadn't learned to be afraid.

My dad had been fending for himself since his early days in the Bronx. He grew up poor with his mother, Sarah, and older sister, Esther, after his father, Abraham, died of malaria when he was nine. But my dad, who was born two and half months premature in 1933 and narrowly missed being smashed by a falling tree branch one day in his stroller, was a scrappy survivor. Weaned on stickball and Woody Guthrie, he was exacting but sensitive, musical and argumentative, a tall, bearded intellectual in black-rimmed glasses. He prided himself on being a tough New York Jew, born in the Bronx but raised for a time in Palestine, where his father worked as a contractor and his cousin was the second prime minister of Israel, Moshe Sharett.

Dad played folk songs in Greenwich Village and, skipping a grade, studied his way up the ranks of two of the city's most competitive schools: the Bronx High School of Science, and City College of New York. It was at CCNY where he discovered anthropology, a burgeoning social science that was not just a career but also, as he often told me, a way of looking at the world, participating and observing. Perhaps it had something to do with how displaced he felt after his father suddenly died at sea. My dad told me he had no memories of his life before the year his father died. The traumatic loss had somehow erased his data. Anthropology allowed him to explore a fundamental question of his life: how the culture of a people, particularly oppressed peoples, survives.

One night in 1958 at a party while completing his master's in anthropology at the University of Arizona, a young woman asked him for a light, and he decided he couldn't survive without her. Her name was Lorraine, a raven-haired Minneapolitan with movie star looks who was passing through on her way to California. Rainy, as she was known by family and friends, was the youngest of three children of a successful attorney, Sam, and a homemaker, Ann.

She'd become enamored of jazz music and, while working at a

jazz record distribution company, befriended many artists and musicians (including pianist Dave Brubeck, who dedicated his song "Sweet Lorraine" to her when he was playing in town). This world of music and adventure appealed to her more than the provincial life at the University of Minnesota and so, at the age of twenty-four, she left for California, where a friend and a new future awaited.

The wonderful thing about chasing freedom—whether on a bus to California or a bike through the woods—is that you never know what you will find. What my mother found, during a stop in Tucson to stay with her brother's family, was my dad. Meeting him at the party, he seemed exotic yet familiar, a New York intellectual who knew both union songs and the best place in town for bagels. Now that he was in the Southwest, my dad had taken to faded jeans and turquoise belt buckles, the folk songs of Mexican singer Miguel Aceves Mejia, and looked like a beatnik cowboy. They fell hard, and quickly, harmonizing together as my dad strummed Pete Seeger songs on his nylon-stringed guitar. He confessed that a mutual friend had told him that if he ever met Rainy from Minneapolis, they would get married. Just a week after meeting, he got down on one knee and proposed.

Together they sang folk songs in living room hootenannies and, after moving to Chapel Hill, North Carolina, where my dad was in graduate school, joined early civil rights sit-ins. Freedom and revolution were in the air, and Dad cut a single of the mountain ballad "Old Joe Clark" with a buddy under the name Mike and Gil from Chapel Hill. In 1960, while pregnant with her first child, my mother turned her activism to women's rights—particularly, the rights of mothers and families in childbirth. At the time, mothers were being drugged in delivery rooms, their husbands banned from entering, and their babies born limp from the anesthetic. The doctors prided themselves on delivering quiet, albeit sedated, babies.

But my mom saw another way, when she read a book published in 1959 called *Thank You, Dr. Lamaze*. It described a technique—popularized by a French obstetrician, Fernand Lamaze, in Europe—that taught women to breathe their way through delivery in lieu of sedation. In America, it was still a relatively unknown and radical method.

For Andy's birth, my mom refused anesthetic and breathed through the labor, just as she had taught herself to do. "I know what you're doing," her doctor told her. "Keep it up." Empowered, she decided to take on the largely conservative birth industry—which favored speedy and predictable deliveries—by teaching women how to enjoy and experience on their own what at the time was called "natural childbirth."

The next year, she and my dad were on a boat with one-year-old Andy, bound for Israel, where my dad had arranged to research and write his PhD dissertation on Jews who had emigrated from the Cochin region of India. They moved into a small, bare concrete home with an outhouse and no hot water. It was in Mesilat Zion, a moshav—a cooperative agricultural community. The Cochin embraced the young family like their own. For my parents, it was a magical time of new experiences and adventure. My father spent his days researching and writing; my mother, tending to Andy and visiting with relatives. There in Israel, they conceived their second child, Jonathan.

3

ANDY WAS only two years older than Jon, an age difference that, as most siblings know, is both a blessing and a curse. You're close enough in age to be friends, sharing common references and interests. But you're also close enough to be rivals. In the early years following Jon's birth, however, the sibling rivalries were still far away. Instead, Andy and Jon enjoyed the playfulness of camaraderie amid the excitement of a young family still finding its roots.

At first, it seemed that the roots might lead them back to Tucson. After finishing his PhD research in Israel and teaching briefly at the University of Houston, my father had planned to return to complete his PhD at Chapel Hill. My dad had always been outspoken about his support of Israel and, while at the University of North Carolina at Chapel Hill, butted heads with a powerful, anti-Israel professor. The next thing my dad knew, he was informed that he couldn't come back. Devastated and angry, he told my mother he was considering giving up his pursuit of the PhD and just settling for his master's. But my mother reassured him that he'd survive, and thrive. "You can't quit," she said. "You have to keep going. Don't let this stop you." So he didn't. A mentor of his at the University of Arizona, Edward Spicer, encouraged him to finish his PhD there.

For Andy, the mid-1960s in Tucson were an idyllic time with Jon, a spry boy with fiery red hair inherited from my mother's father, Sam. Though my dad was hard at work on his doctorate and writing his dissertation, he made a point to take the family out into the desert whenever he could, packing a lunch of fried chicken, made by my mother from a recipe she'd learned in Chapel Hill. Andy would always remember sitting on the rocks among the cacti at the Saguaro National Monument Park, dipping fried chicken in honey with Jon.

On the days that my dad was writing or teaching, my mom relished her life with her two boys. She took them to theme parks and to visit her brother's family nearby. On Mother's Day, Jon and Andy dressed her in a homemade paper crown and handed her a long paper staff with a star on top to hold. She taught Lamaze to local women when she could, and made the local papers when she was among the first in town to pick up what was then heralded as a new form of recreational exercise: jogging.

But, as with any struggling family, there were challenges. Money was tight. The future was unknown. My dad was prone to worrying about finances, and how he'd support his children and send them to college. He was also besieged with a rare form of severe headaches called cluster headaches, which struck at random and left one side of his face temporarily paralyzed as if he had had a stroke. The headaches lasted for around twenty minutes or so and defied medical treatment. He was told to avoid alcohol, though occasionally he downed a shot or two of his favorite mescal. Other than that, he just had to hope the headaches wouldn't debilitate him at inopportune moments, and ride them out when they hit.

The stress would wear him down at times, and he could be strict, snapping with frustration over mounting bills or a messy house. He was never abusive, physically or mentally, but had that New Yorker trait of being able to scream at someone and then, minutes later, scream that he wasn't screaming. My mother worried that sometimes my dad was too hard on the boys.

With his PhD soon complete, my father accepted a position at the State University of New York at Brockport, where I was born in 1968. My mother would never forget bringing me home in the middle of winter to see Jon and Andy's eager faces pressed against the window. In the haste of delivery, they had forgotten to pack me baby clothes, so I arrived in a thin blue hospital gown. Eight years younger than Andy and six years younger than Jon, I became the family plaything. Andy and Jon delighted in toting me around, and scooting down the stairs beside me. My father would play songs on his guitar while my mom accompanied him on piano.

In the summer of 1969, my parents celebrated their fourteenth wedding anniversary. I have a small black-and-white picture of the five of us around the cake. My father, with a trim, dark beard and black-framed glasses, leans against my mother, who is holding me as I laugh while they blow out the candles. Andy and Jon are seated alongside, smiling. Jon's hands are pressed together, midclap. Our family of five is complete.

4

IN 1970 my father accepted a job as professor at the University of South Florida in Tampa, which had an up-and-coming anthropology department. The prospect of moving to Florida thrilled my parents. We were northern Jews making the pilgrimage south just like so many of our leathery forebearers. But, like many, they equated Florida with South Florida. As a kid, my mother had gone on vacation to Miami Beach with her family, and still cherished the memories of lounging on the white sands. My dad had an uncle Sid, who was a nightclub pianist in Miami Beach, performing under the less Semitic stage name Mickey O'Toole. The prospect of raising their three boys in the warmth—no snow to shovel, no ice to clear—delighted my parents, who hoped this might be the last in what had been a long string of moves.

But it didn't take long after they arrived in Tampa to realize this wasn't a city of liberal New Yorkers. While looking at one home to buy, they noticed a grimy toilet in the garage. The realtor told them it was for the "*shvarzte*" help—a word that had not lost its fashion here despite this being 1970. A popular restaurant chain in town was called Sambo's. The walls inside had paintings of the restaurant's mascot, Sambo, a little black boy in a watermelon field.

Though steeped in Cuban history and billed as the "cigar capitol of the world," Tampa was still rural, and felt more like Georgia than Florida. It represented the paradox of the Sunshine State: the farther north you go, the more southern it gets. People drove pickup trucks in Tampa, spoke with southern accents, chewed tobacco, and bought rusty tools at flea markets. The Florida State Fair, held in nearby Plant City since 1904, wasn't just an annual diversion, it represented a way of life. The Tampa Bay area was America's capital of carnies and circus performers. Sarasota had the headquarters for the famous Ringling Bros. and Barnum & Bailey circus, and Gibsonton was the year-round home for the largest concentration of self-described sideshow "freaks" on the planet, such as Monkey Girl and Lobster Boy—the latter of whom, a man born with clawlike hands and feet, later became notorious for murdering his daughter's fiancé.

As my parents were finding their way in this new city, they soon faced a new challenge of their own. Something seemed off with Jon. Though playful, bright, and affectionate, he seemed to have trouble processing information. He found it difficult to understand basic instructions and sometimes jumbled words. One time at synagogue, the rabbi posed a question to the children, and Jon gave a nonsensical response that left others feeling uncomfortable.

My brother's struggles created tension between my parents. My dad put a high value on intellectual prowess. As someone who had used his brain to pull himself out of the Bronx, he feared what might be in store for Jon—especially when Andy and I were doing fine. What Jon needed, they agreed, was the right school. But after looking around town at different prospects, my parents grew discouraged when they went to one place where the students were in uniforms and being ordered to sit up straight. They thought this would be too much for Jon, who they felt needed more nurturing and support. And that's just what they found when they drove up to Independent Day School, a small private school on the north side of town.

IDS, as it was nicknamed, seemed hatched from a hippie dream. There were long-haired kids sitting in trees, and teachers wearing faded jeans and beards that rivaled my dad's—which now hung down low on his chest alongside his long dark hair. The entire school, which ran from kindergarten through seventh grade, had fewer than a hundred students. The campus spread over eight leafy acres of ponds, creeks, and cypress and citrus trees. A former orange grove, IDS teemed with wild peacocks—an especially surreal sight in the suburbs. The birds had been brought to the area by a farmer in the 1920s to ward off trespassers. In a promotional brochure, IDS cheekily referred to the birds as the school's "watchdogs."

Instead of the usual square brick buildings, classes at IDS took place in a half dozen circular brown pods and, for the sixth- and seventh-graders, a giant yellow geodesic dome in the fashion of Buckminster Fuller. The Dome, as it was nicknamed, and the "Domies" inside, represented the pantheon of IDS-ness. Students aspired to the Dome and the day that they would become Domies. Walking inside the three-story-high building felt like entering a moon colony of Deadheads. Everyone seemed to have long, straight hair—the men and women, boys and girls—and some shade of bell-bottoms with patches of peace signs and rainbows.

Instead of orderly desks and chairs, the room was a jumble of metal folding chairs and wood-paneled tables.

Inside the Dome, a colorful banner read "Happiness is like a butterfly: the more you chase it, the more it eludes you," with the word *butterfly* represented by an illustration. The twenty-five-foot-high ceiling consisted of white insulation foam, porous but firm enough to catch the pointy end of a pencil chucked by some slack-jawed middle schooler and leave the pencil hanging there. Before long, all kinds of pointy supplies—protractors, rulers, and, most treacherously, sharp-tipped metal compasses—protruded from the entire ceiling. Kids would be sitting cross-legged in a circle discussing Frank Lloyd Wright with an earnest hippie instructor when a compass or pencil would loosen and plummet stealthily to the floor—or upon a head, arm, or lap.

The school was as groovy as white suburban 1970s groove could be. Its mission statement declared that "a happy child who is given respect as a unique human allowed to fulfill his needs to play, to investigate, and to be himself, is more open to learning than a child who is unhappy, tense, and fearful." This philosophy had come from the founders, two grad students at USF trained in gifted education. Classes were designed around the British Infant Model, blending two grades as one and allowing these students to progress at their own pace.

In a symbolic gesture, someone removed the ringer of an old bell left on the property from its days as a farm because, as a caption beneath a picture of it in the yearbook noted, "traditional school bells never ring at un-traditional IDS." This sort of holistic consciousness, or conscientiousness, extended to the weekly field trips, called "community classes." As well as going to the local library, IDS students visited the local slaughterhouse to learn how meat was produced.

IDS attracted children of professors like my dad, as well as lawyers and artists around town. One kid came to school every day by paddling his canoe across the lake. Another had parents who let her choose her own name. She chose "Blackbird," for the Beatles song; before that she was just called Girl. Students not only climbed the many trees, but also they spent classes there perched on branches. To earn money, kids would get paid to clean lettuce.

For my parents, the school felt like a progressive oasis, and they eagerly signed up Andy and Jon to attend. They bought a small ranch house with a red-tile roof close enough by that the boys could walk to school. A creek separated our backyard from the campus. When people would say how annoying it must be to hear the screaming kids all day back there, my mother told them that she loved hearing the children's voices.

Jon and Andy were happy to join the chorus of these free-range kids. They ran around barefoot, built wigwams from fallen palm fronds, and gathered tadpoles at the lake during recess. The citrus groves became a steady part of the diet, and entertainment regimen. During softball games, the pitcher might clandestinely slip a grapefruit into her glove, lobbing it to the unsuspecting hitter, who, to his surprise, would smack it into a pulpy blast. To crack down on orange fights, teachers made a rule that any fruit thrown, even the rotten ones, had to be eaten.

Andy had taken up photography, and would shoot pictures of the kids forming a human pyramid up the Dome. Jon and his friends spent recess playing soccer or shoving one another into the pond—a convenient excuse for Jon to run home for a change of clothes. He might come back over the newly constructed bridge on the main road or, if he was feeling more like Huck Finn, balance-beam across the creek on one of the few wooden planks positioned there by adolescent explorers. After school, Jon and Andy would head up to the other nearby school to play H-O-R-S-E on the basketball court.

Jon became known as a quiet but thoughtful boy with a compassionate streak. One time, one of my brother's friends fell from a tree, and Jon came to his aid. "You're okay," he told him, "just breathe deep. You got the wind knocked out of you." Another time, Andy fell into a pond while looking for turtles and Jon readily helped fish him out.

But while Jon seemed to be finding his place among the kids and the teachers, he still struggled to get by in class. When the teacher dictated simple sentences for the class to write down, Jon's paper would often be missing words. If the teacher said, "The quick brown fox jumps over the lazy dog," he might just write "the quick fox dog." Jon's grades began to plummet, along with his self-esteem. At home, there were more frequent conflicts with Andy—like fighting over who got to sit in the front seat of the car. My parents sought the help of a psychologist, who established behavior modification plans, keeping tabs on the refrigerator as each boy completed chores so that he could earn the front seat.

The psychologist determined that Jon was suffering from an auditory memory deficit disorder—a sort of aural dyslexia that jumbled the words he heard. Seeking help, my parents sent him to a speech therapist for weekly sessions. Jon, like many ten-year-olds, put up a fight about going to see her after school but stuck it out. The speech therapist would read sentences to Jon and tell him to draw a blank line when he came to word that he couldn't remember. They would then go back over the sentences until the blanks were filled. Before long, Jon began to improve. His scores jumped a full two or three grades in the span of eight months. My parents felt relieved as he brightened and gained confidence. Jon relaxed more during his visits with his speech therapist and began joking around with her. One afternoon, he brought her a gift: a small jar of dyed sand he'd layered like a rainbow.

5

THE HELICOPTER circled faster and faster, cutting the air with whirring blades. Down below, the astronaut drifted alone in a bright orange raft on a deep blue sea. His orange capsule bobbed nearby. The whirlybird lowered down, angling to pick up the astronaut and bring him to safety.

It was not long after we had moved to our new house in Tampa, and Jon and I were playing with our favorite toy, the VertiBird. Created by Mattel, the battery-powered toy promised "safe flying fun," as the box read, by letting us "pilot real copter missions!" The small orange plastic copter with black blades was attached to a square white and yellow base by a long white spindle. To control the whirlybird, we pulled back or forth on two levers: a throttle and pitch control. The harder we pressed, the faster the bird went, occasionally careening into the blue shag carpet below.

The toy's theme was inspired by the Apollo moon landings: you had to save the astronaut and his capsule from sinking. This rescue was achieved by lowering the chopper just enough to maneuver the skyhook through a tiny hoop on each of the scattered parts. The breeze and buzzing sound from the tiny blades were hypnotic, and I would twirl the helicopter as fast as it could go, speeding it recklessly into a storm, as Jon laughed harder than he could tell me to stop. Occasionally I'd ignore the sticker warning on the control unit to "Be a Safe Operator/Keep Behind Controls" and get smacked in the side of my head by the dull plastic blades. We found that hilarious.

Freedom and flight were the themes of Jon's bedroom. It started with the VertiBird and extended to his walls. Wallpaper was everything at the time, a projection of our personalities, as if we'd swallowed a lightbulb that shone through our skin and tattooed the walls with our dreams. Our dreams—and our wallpaper—came in primary-colored pop art that was fashionable at the time. In my room, three walls were papered in red, yellow, white, and blue vertical stripes. The wall opposite my bed featured soldiers on horseback with faces like playing card Jacks. If I stared long enough at the soldiers while I was falling asleep, they seemed to move. Andy, now a studious and aspiring thirteen-year-old musician, had a giant red arrow sweeping down his wall along with the words *Start Here*. He positioned his brown-sparkle drum set at the tip of the arrow.

Jon's wallpaper was the trippiest of all, like some Roy Lichtenstein collage of illustrations or a scramble of images from *Yellow Submarine*. It featured a jumble of street signs—pedestrian crosswalk, yield, honk for curb service—floating over abstract swirls of colors, black-and-white-checkered optical illusion globes, and Hang Ten footprints. A sexy blonde woman wore a dress of yellow feathers that spelled the phrase "Not Now Darling." The whole thing seemed like hippie hieroglyphics with a Freudian subtext. Alongside the woman was the face of a stern, mustachioed cop pointing his finger, with a stop sign beside him.

But there was no stopping my and Jon's imaginations from taking off. When I padded barefoot into the room in my pajamas and flopped down on the shag, I had come to fly. Jon would briskly open his drawer and pull out our bible: a small black flight manual. It had been given to us by Mr. Landman, a friend of our parents who was an air force pilot. The book was even more cryptic than Jon's wallpaper, full of numbers and codes and diagrams and maps and suggestions of another world—the world we flew into every time we pressed on the VertiBird levers.

I took extra interest in the VertiBird excursions because I was still too young to venture very far for real. The farthest I'd get would be the end of the sidewalk on my Big Wheel tricycle, but I had plenty of tantalizing woods to explore. Our house had been built on the lot of a tree nursery. The backyard teemed with podocarpus trees, which had thin, pointy leaves and small sour purple berries. Neighbors tore down their trees to build swimming pools, but my parents told the bulldozer drivers to keep away from ours.

My brothers and I were thankful the trees remained. We lost ourselves there, tunneling into the paths to play hide and seek. We had company in the backyard: a colony of pet turtles. They began arriving one day when one of us brought home a yellow-and-green-shelled box turtle found outside. Then came another, and another. To accommodate the growing herd, my dad dug a shallow hole in the back and filled it with concrete to make a pond. He fixed a green wire fence around the perimeter. Word got out, and other kids began bringing by errant turtles: snappers and tortoises. Soon we had nearly a dozen. We became known as the turtle family. The turtles were a great incentive for throwing out the garbage. Every night, my brothers and I fought over who would get to dump the half-eaten vegetables into their pen.

A creek behind the turtle pond led to an even wider and wilder world to explore. Because our house backed up against the woods, the paths seemed endless. After school and on weekends, we'd see skinny, long-haired kids in cutoffs and T-shirts dart by on their urgent adventures. Where they were going, I had no idea, but I was jealous that Andy and Jon were old enough to join them. I imagined them off in some incredible secret place, like the cove from my favorite TV show, *Sigmund and the Sea Monster*. The show was about this boy who, while off on his own neighborhood adventure, discovered a cave of friendly sea monsters: Sigmund, the nice one, and his mischievous brothers Burp and Slurp.

The sea monsters were just actors on some Hollywood lot, sweating inside big, rubbery green costumes, but I was still young enough to suspend disbelief. The fact that the show's hero had red hair and was named Johnny made it even more compelling. Maybe my own red-haired brother Jon would find Sigmund beyond the creek and bring him home to play with our turtles and VertiBird, I imagined. Kids spoke of secret caves in the woods across the street from our house, not far from the 7-Eleven.

6

NINETEEN SEVENTY-THREE was a peak year for my family. My parents both turned forty. After spending most of their adulthood moving from city to city, they could finally get used to calling Tampa home.

My dad was living his dreams at work. His PhD dissertation was published as a book, *Immigrants from India to Israel*, his first. Someone snapped a photo of him in his office, holding up the book with his left hand while reaching over his head and playfully pointing at it with his right. His hair and beard were long and black, and he wore tinted aviator shades. He looked like a cross between Allen Ginsberg and Tommy Chong (a comparison that he prided himself on). One of my pre-K finger paintings—a Halloween-themed piece of thick-limbed stick figures and a smudgy witch—hung on his wall behind him.

Under his leadership as *chairperson* (the more egalitarian term he used instead of *chairman*), the department was receiving international attention for launching the first master's program in applied anthropology in the world. Applied anthropology took academics out of the ivory tower and into the field, exploring ways in which they could apply their training to practical problems, from urban planning to public health. The master's program, which would begin in 1974, kept very much in line with my dad's history of social activism; at the same time, it was considered heretical by those who thought that anthros—as my dad and his colleagues referred to themselves—should stay in the classroom.

But it fit the radical times. Not long before, students at my dad's university, USF, and others had staged a massive protest nearby that blocked a major intersection and ended with local police firing tear gas into the crowd. The Watergate scandal was now dominating the news. A peace treaty had been reached in Vietnam, though the horrors of the conflict still lingered.

While my dad fought for his program, my mother, who worked part-time, was fighting to empower women in childbirth. Nurses invited her to come to the hospital to teach Lamaze to their mothers, but when one doctor found out, he wrote my mother an angry letter, stating, "You have no right going into my hospital in a sterile area." My mom didn't back down. "I didn't plan this," she told him. "Your nurses invited me."

A local reporter came to write a story on my mom's classes, the first of their kind in Tampa. Soon more nurses began contacting her, one influential woman in particular. "She said, 'You're here, I know what you're doing, I heard about Lamaze,'" my mother recalled. "'We're going to back you up.'" As my mom held more and more classes at our home, Andy, Jon, and I got used to opening the front door to pregnant women. My dad once joked that the other men in the neighborhood must have been impressed—or dismayed—by all the expectant mothers with pillows arriving at our house.

Because my parents were so engaged in their causes, they felt an even greater sense of community with their colleagues and friends. Parties at our house became regular occurrences, especially because my dad had to host visiting faculty when they passed through town. I spent many nights weaving through blue-jeaned legs and paisley dresses, as Cat Stevens records played on the turntable. Outside on the patio, I'd spy small clusters of artists, professors, actresses, and teachers passing joints and laughing. The celebrations peaked in March 1973 with Andy's bar mitzvah. By thirteen, he had already found his passion, playing trumpet, and was showing exceptional skill in his school bands. Compared with Jon and me, Andy had an incredible sense of dedication and could spend hours in his room practicing his horn.

That summer, as my parents celebrated another wedding anniversary, Jon was finding his place too. He was attending Camp Keystone in a patch of woods fifteen minutes from our house. With his school troubles fading behind him, my brother reveled in the freedom of camp, playing soccer, reading comic books, and having water pistol fights. He recorded him and his friends on his cassette tape recorder, showing off his Donald Duck impression. They photographed one another shirtless, shooting birds with both hands, their middle fingers raised. Jon was growing up.

For Jon's eleventh birthday, September 13, 1973, the family took him to his favorite pizza place, Shakey's, where he joked around in the birthday hat with his friends as he relished having an entire pizza to himself. Back home, Jon opened our front door to find a delivery man standing alongside a shiny green Schwinn bicycle. It was a gift from my parents, who knew how much he loved riding his bike. With him growing taller and lankier, they figured it was time for the next size up. Jon eagerly took the bike for a spin, pedaling down the driveway to the street, feeling the familiar rush of wind and motion. My parents ran outside with a camera and snapped a black-and-white photo of him there, the same kind of picture that has been taken by parents thousands of times before and since: a happy child riding a new bike for the first time.

7

OCTOBER 28, 1973, began like any other Sunday. Andy woke up early to go to a youth group meeting at our synagogue on the other side of town. He sometimes carpooled with a local teenager whom he never really liked. He and Jon had made a game out of his dread, hiding by the window and peaking outside as they heard the car pull up. On this day, they let their inside joke go further than usual, and, unbeknownst to my parents, pretended they didn't hear the door when the boy came knocking. Andy figured my mom would just drive him instead, which she did.

But it was going to be a busy day. That night, my parents were hosting a dinner for the social club at our synagogue, Havorah. Though immersed in university and IDS life, they were hoping to build up their community at shul, and this dinner was the start. After Andy and Mom left, Jon went outside to mow the lawn. The grass, even in the fall, grew quickly and thickly, and my dad encouraged Andy and Jon to take turns mowing to earn their allowance.

By around noon, when Jon was done, he asked my dad if it was okay to bike to the 7-Eleven to buy some candy. It was the same ride he'd taken countless times, just like all the other kids in the neighborhood. My dad said okay and settled into his big black chair in the den to catch the Minnesota Vikings–Los Angeles Rams game on TV, a formidable battle of two undefeated football teams.

Jon slipped on his red, white, and blue Hush Puppies and went into his room, where he took a dollar from his wallet. Then he headed out to the garage and grabbed his old red bike. As he pedaled down the driveway and turned right onto the sidewalk toward the woods, I trailed after him until he stopped. We had that conversation about the candy I wanted, the Snappy Gator Gum. And then he was gone.

8

I only have six memories before the day Jon disappeared, and they come in this order: (1) climbing out of my crib; (2) playing a McDonald's game with Andy and Jon, who both laughed when I chose to be the villainous Hamburglar; (3) riding a Big Wheel down my sidewalk; (4) riding a Big Wheel at Mrs. Quinn's day care; (5) playing with the pilot book with Jon; and (6) playing with the VertiBird with Jon. But beginning with my last conversation with Jon on the sidewalk, several more memories rapidly piled up that week.

I am on the sidewalk talking with a police officer. He's asking me to describe what Jon was wearing. "A brown muscle shirt," I say. "Shorts."

A kind older woman, Marge Bernstein, takes me to buy Silly Putty. I return to find a lot of people at my house, including the police.

I'm inside the house when the door opens to another police officer. He's big and serious. He says something, and I run into Andy's bedroom. Andy is sitting on the edge of his bed, forlorn.

"They found him!" I shout. Andy looks up numbly. I follow him back to the foyer, where, overhearing the conversation, I realize they haven't found Jon at all. They've found only his bike. I feel terrible for telling Andy they had found our brother instead. But if Jon isn't in the woods, where is he?

Sometime later, I'm in the kitchen, and the transistor radio is on. The person on the radio is talking about our family. My mom and Andy are sitting at the white round kitchen table, and Andy is comforting her, as she is crying. I say something about how at least our name was on the radio, as if that's somehow cool and uplifting. I feel confused and terrible as my mom continues to cry, and Andy, his arm around her shoulder, helps her out of the room.

At another point, I'm tossing the black flight book that Jon and I played with into an empty grave.

Then my memories of that week stop.

Part 2

9

I DON'T RECALL when or how I learned that Jon had been murdered. All I knew was that something very awful and very public had happened to my family, and that Jon wasn't coming back. It felt like being cast in a Grimm's fairy tale made real: a boy went into the woods where he met monsters and never returned. But pages of my book were torn and missing.

Eventually a sketchy narrative lodged in my mind. While biking through the woods, Jon had been hit in the head with a lead pipe and abducted by two men. He suffocated in the trunk of their car. He was missing for a week before he was found dead.

But, being so young, I struggled to process truth from fantasy, and lacked the courage or wherewithal to ask more questions. The full story of what happened to Jon remained a mystery. And it was a mystery that I had to answer for myself. Along the way, I discovered something I didn't know I was seeking; the answer to the question that almost everyone had for us when they heard our story. It was one that applies not only to our rare experience but also to anyone suffering a loss: How do you go on?

I began seeking the answers at the spot where the future ended: on the sidewalk in front of my parents' house. It was about thirty years after Jon had died. I was visiting from New York City, where I was working as a writer, and living with my wife and three-year-old daughter. On this sunny, warm winter morning, I had taken my daughter outside to ride a new tricycle for the first time. The bike was pink, and had pink and white streamers on the handlebars. I helped her guide it out of the garage, and down the small hill of the cracked concrete driveway. The Spanish-tiled roof had long since broken away and been replaced by flat shingles. The once barren yard had filled in with thick, lush green bushes and pink azaleas. The wild peacocks from nearby IDS had turned into multitudes, and now lazed around my parents' lawn.

We set the bike to rest at the first level spot on the sidewalk that ran to the end of the block at the street by the woods. A few homes had been built across the street years before, but many of the cypress trees remained, taller now, and dripping with long gray tangles of Spanish moss, like the beards of thin giants. In the years following Jon's death, I never ventured into the woods. I didn't have the courage or desire, and my parents didn't want me going there anyway. But the woods remained a looming reminder of a shadowy past; its trees had borne witness to Jon pedaling over the palm fronds beneath them to the 7-Eleven on the other side.

Standing there with my daughter, I saw the two moments overlaying, like film strips playing over each other to form double images. There was me as the little kid standing next to my brother on his bike, and me as the grown-up standing next to my daughter on hers. I thought about how much had changed, how the freedom that Jon had in his final moments seemed so endangered, if not extinct, for children now. The last free generation of kids had let their fears take away their kids' freedom.

As my daughter climbed eagerly onto her seat, I wondered what most parents wonder: How I would find the strength to give her the freedom she needed? How could I let her go into the world knowing that anything could happen? How could I survive if anything did? When I asked my parents how they did it, they said they always wanted me to get the most out of life. But now, as my daughter wiggled her feet on her pedals, I had no idea how they could have possibly endured. I had to venture into the woods of time and memory, where the mysteries remained.

10

THE PATH of a child is broken. The memories that pave the way come in fragments. I could look down on each block as if it were some kind of flickering screen, short loops of static and film from some other life. One by one, they would lead me through the shadows.

The first one starts when Marge Bernstein, the woman who had tended to me the week my brother was missing, pulled into my driveway with me after taking me to buy a Slinky toy. My parents were standing in the doorway, and I ran eagerly up the sidewalk to show them what I got. I could feel them staring at me in a way I didn't understand, the look of surprise on their faces. As I felt a soggy weight beneath my shoes, I realized why: the sidewalk to our house had just been poured with fresh concrete, and I had unwittingly stomped through it, leaving a trail of thick gray footprints behind me. Sometime later, Andy took a broken stick and scrawled letters and numbers in the wet cement. On the left side of the sidewalk, he wrote *David K '73*, on the right, *Andy K '73*. Jon's name, I knew, would have been in the empty space in between.

Next comes the memory at the Jewish Community Center in

Tampa, where my preschool teacher, a family friend, is talking to us about Jon's death not long after he died. We sit cross-legged on the thick multicolored rug where the other four-year-olds and I always gathered for story time, but this is a story I can't understand. I don't know how much she told us, or what we asked. But I remember the unsettling feeling that came with knowing this story was about my family. I felt transparent and exposed, a character in a story that the adults understood better than the kids did. It was a strange sense of celebrity that would linger for years; a spotlight that was warm with compassion but unwanted.

On the ground of the woods is another flickering screen. It shows me in the office of a gentle man with kind eyes who gives me a shiny cold can of Sprite—an entire can to myself, which I'd never had before—and asks me to draw a picture of my house. This is Dr. Ball, the same psychologist who'd treated Jon. I take a crayon and begin drawing as he watches thoughtfully. I draw the square of the building. Two tiny windows with perpendicular lines. A door. A walkway. As I sit there on the brown leather couch, I watch him study the drawing in his hands, the way he tilts his head and appraises my work. I remember feeling skeptical and angry. What could he possibly learn about me from looking at that picture?

Whatever details I'd been told about Jon's death didn't stick. This begged more questions: Who killed him? Why did they do it? How did he end up in a car? Where was he taken? What else happened? How was he found? Though, looking back now, I don't know if those questions even entered my head at the time. I just remember lying on my bed's fuzzy orange blanket, and kicking the wall that separated my room from Jon's over and over again as hard as I could while I screamed. I did that for what seemed like hours, and the tantrums became commonplace. The doctor prescribed tranquilizers.

We were once a family in our own solar system, like any family, and then we were cast out of orbit, each of us drifting into our own time and space, occasionally feeling the gravity of one another's pull. I can see my mother coming into my room after another tantrum of mine and rubbing my back, singing a lullaby to comfort me. I don't see my father. I don't see Andy. And before long, my mother isn't there, and my room is silent and dark. Outside my room, there's a windowless hallway with a yellow shag carpet. My parents are in their room at one end. Andy is in his at the other. Jon's room is empty. The doors are shut.

11

ANDY'S DOOR, like each of ours, was pine colored with darker swirls of wood stain. The doorknob was mottled brass. In the middle of the knob was a thin slit that, I discovered, would pop open if I slid a butter knife inside it and twisted it to the right. Andy's room was often locked, so I resorted to my own means.

He was going through what he would later recall as his own private hell. He and Jon had a different relationship than Jon and I did. They knew each other longer. I was the last to the party. They'd played cowboy in Houston, dipped fried chicken in honey in the Arizona desert, poured their milk down the drain when my parents weren't looking. They shared joyous times in Tampa, riding the log flume at Busch Gardens, playing basketball after school. But there were fights. Jealousies. The standard skirmishes over territory and love.

But imagine being in the middle of a fight with your friend or sibling or whomever, and then all of a sudden the person vanishes. That's what happened to Andy. Jon was there and then he was gone. Midday, midresolve. And Andy, being thirteen, was old enough to intellectualize this and process it. He could stand in the hallway outside Jon's door and remember the conversations they had, the shouting, the storming off. And then nothing. An absence. A sinkhole that opened on a Sunday afternoon and swallowed Jon whole.

Andy felt guilty. He thought about the time our cousin was coming over, and how he wanted to play with his red sailboat with Michael, just the two of them, and how disappointed he was when Jon came along. He felt terrible for having tried to ditch his brother. His belly still bore a little scar from when he'd fallen into the pond and Jon pulled him out—evidence of what his little brother had done for him.

Andy felt nagged by magical thinking. Some notion that if he had just done something differently, Jon would still be alive. He replayed the moment from that morning when he and Jon stood at the window and pretended not to hear the doorbell when Andy's ride came for the synagogue. It was a happy moment; they were playing. Later Andy saw Jon and me on the living room floor, laughing hysterically over something he couldn't recall. Then he was off with my mother, who had to take him to synagogue, since he'd missed his ride.

This shift in fate ate away at Andy. What if he hadn't missed his ride? Then Mom would have been home that morning, and Jon, perhaps, would have been doing something with her instead of riding off into the woods. At first, when Andy came back from the synagogue, he didn't make anything of Jon's still not being home. Andy had gone off into those woods himself many times, just like most kids in the area. That afternoon, Andy had plans of his own. He grabbed his bike and headed off with his friend to a nearby mall. When he came back, he saw the police cars and crowds outside our home. "Jon's missing," my mother told him. "He didn't come home."

Andy joined the search party with my dad. They went into the woods across the street, which was thick with fallen palm fronds and brush. Around him, he saw all kinds of people, both familiar and strange: professors, students, classmates, bikers, farmers, police. When we'd moved to Tampa, he felt wary of Southerners, but now, as these strangers searched beside him, he felt a connection that would stay with him for the rest of his life.

But he also felt tremendous fear. Andy had been through here so many times, but now it felt so foreboding. As urgent as he felt out there searching for Jon, the reality of finding Jon terrified him. By the time night fell that first evening, Andy felt sure that Jon had been kidnapped and killed. Though I remembered seeing him look hopeful when I told him, wrongly, that they'd found Jon that afternoon, Andy recalled later that he had long lost any hope at all. He could see in my face that I still had it, but for him it was gone, and he felt no surprise to learn they had found only Jon's bike.

The week unfolded like a nightmare for Andy. He would remember the phone calls to the house, each of which my dad had to answer in case it was a genuine lead. Many of the calls were pranks from vicious thrill seekers, either claiming they had information about Jon's whereabouts or pretending to be Jon himself.

He also would remember the psychic: a woman in a long, flowing robe who took one of Jon's shoes and focused on it like some portal into his whereabouts. When she walked into Andy's bedroom, she told him, "I sense hope in here." He wanted to punch her.

But while Andy endured the horror, he didn't forget his feeling of responsibility to his other little brother: me. Jon had gone missing just three days before Halloween, after all, and the neighborhood was still decorated for the holiday. Andy hadn't been back to school during the search, and had no idea who, if anyone, still planned on going trick-or-treating when a killer could be on the loose. But he was determined to give me a sense of normalcy in a reality that was anything but. So on Halloween, he helped me suit up into my costume, one that neither he nor I would remember, though probably one of those store-bought masks with a rubber band around the back. Maybe Casper the Friendly Ghost. Then he took me outside, and we went house to house as candy filled my bag.

That night would prove too much of a blur for Andy to remember our neighbors' reactions to seeing us at their doors. But one can only imagine the moment: two brothers trick-or-treating while the other is missing, and how sad and scary and poignant the whole thing must have been. Decades later, long after we had become the closest of brothers and friends, I told Andy how much I'd always love him and appreciate him for what he did for me that night.

At some point, the blur of people and food and police gave way to Andy's memory of being at his friend's house when he got the call that he was going to be picked up. He knew in that moment that something horrible had been discovered. It had been eight days since Jon had vanished. He sat in the car with Dad and the psychologist, Espy Ball, the one who had treated Jon and, later, me. Dr. Ball told him that Jon was dead. That was it, no details for now, just: Jon, dead. Andy felt something inside him shut off, some wall slam down between him and the insanity of what he'd just heard, and, for some time, he stayed that way. When he would hear the knock of my little fist on his door in the weeks to come, I couldn't understand why he was slow to answer.

12

At the opposite end of the hallway from Andy, I would find my parents' door cracked open slightly. Sometimes I would push it cautiously and find my father lying in bed in the throes of a cluster headache. He wore a translucent oxygen mask, which was attached to a tube running to the large green oxygen tank that stood between his bed and a tall wooden dresser. His glasses rested on the bed beside him. Half of his face looked slackened and wet, as if molded poorly from clay.

My father's migraines weren't new or stress related. But it was hard to see him like this, under siege, debilitated by some invisible dark force that I couldn't understand. And when I follow the broken path of those days to my father, this is some of the only footage I see. The headaches. The oxygen tank. The mask. Other times I see him sitting on the patio in the backyard, looking off into the trees as he smoked a cigarette. At some point, I stood by the sliding glass doors and saw him sitting in a chair, a towel around his shoulders as he leaned back with his face to the sun while my mother trimmed his beard.

On Friday nights, I saw him leading us in *Shabbos*. We were conservative Jews—more cultural than religious—but my father loved the ritual and tradition of Judaism. He would stand at the head of the table and crack open his small green siddur, which he had received upon his bar mitzvah in the Bronx. I can't recall if the *Shabbos* dinners subsided in the wake of Jon's death. In my path, the footage plays every Friday night. My mother lighting the candles. My dad singing the prayers from his green siddur. Andy doing the blessing over the bread, me doing the wine. Then the four of us together singing the final prayers before eating roast chicken and matzo ball soup.

But there were nights when during *Shabbos* my father would begin to cry. He would lower his prayer book, and my mother would reach for his hand. Andy might bow his head, waiting for the moment to pass. Nothing was said, as I recall, beyond perhaps my mother saying, "I know." There was nothing to say. And there was silence. So much silence filling the house during all these vignettes. Some of the times when my father would begin to cry, I can see him walking off into his room to shut the door behind him. I didn't sense that it was because he was ashamed of his emotions but, rather, that perhaps the emotions were too much for him to experience among us. I wondered if somehow he was protecting me from the things I didn't know.

And there were so many things I didn't know about what he had experienced that week. I didn't know that my mother had come home from carpooling Andy to ask him where Jon was, and for him to tell her he'd gone to the store and hadn't returned yet. I didn't know at what point this normal childhood excursion turned into panic and fear when Jon was away too long. I didn't know when or how the police found out; or that my father had gone off into the woods with Andy to search; or that he endured the phone calls from strangers, the cranks, the concerned; or that he had given weary interviews to dogged reporters, and gone on the local TV news to plead for information about his missing son. I didn't know how he reacted when Espy Ball and the sheriff came to tell him the news that Jon was dead.

The death temporarily derailed what had been the rapid ascent of my father's career. It was the fall of 1973, the academic year having just begun. His anthropology department, which he chaired, was ramping up for its graduate program in applied anthropology to begin the next fall. But for untold weeks, that was gone. The professors and students would fill our house, offering whatever they could to support us. The house was full so often—full of food, full of love, stretches of silence, and tears.

I didn't know that my mother and father had cut a deal with each other. If one of them began to cry, the other would be there for support, and vice versa. They would be there for each other. But it was too painful to talk about Jon. Down the hall, his room remained shut.

13

MY MOTHER would be the one to finally open Jon's door for good. But it would not come easy. The interminable week when Jon was missing had been a nightmarish blur for her. There was the moment she felt something was wrong when she came home to find Jon still away, and the flash of anger toward my father for not having been aware. There was the crush of people in the house, the strange pull of playing hostess to the ones that passed through—friends, strangers, police—and being hosted by these people in her own home, too, when she didn't have the strength. My mother, who'd made a life bringing babies into the world, would be remembered that week for the warmth she showed to the people in our house, the way she made them feel comfortable and welcomed, even those we didn't know.

But there was the horror and the pain, the widening chasm of fear as each day ticked by without Jon coming home. The few moments that I remembered—when the policemen found his bike, when the radio said our name—were lost in the dark swirl of madness that she felt enveloping her, the insanity that crested with the news that her child had been found dead.

But it wasn't only Jon who had died that week. It was something in my mother too. She would look into her bathroom mirror and not recognize her face. She would burst into tears as my father comforted her, and then be comforting him the next moment. She felt at sea, occasionally drifting back to check on Andy and me, to console me during one of my tantrums, or to try to reach Andy, who was pulling further and further away.

She moved through the days and nights, fulfilling her responsibilities as best she could. At some point when Andy returned to school, she would drive him to rehearsals with his school concert band. As she watched him walk into school with his trumpet case, she so wanted to connect with him, to talk about Jon, to have him share, only to see that moment dissipate.

She and my father had been following the psychologist's advice on how best to deal with Andy and me. Within a few weeks of Jon's death, the psychologist thought it was best for him to know the details of the murder, which he shared with Andy himself. As for what, if anything, was shared with me, no one—not me, nor my parents—would recall later. All they could remember was that when the doctor suggested that my frequent outbursts be treated with tranquilizers, they followed his advice.

This was a time when therapy for children wasn't common, and even my parents, for all they knew, didn't know enough to have me in treatment. But my mother would hug me hard, like Jon used to hug—he was known for his tight grip, consciously transferring his energy to me—thinking, *David will hug like Jon did.* But she knew I was fighting demons of my own. One day I drew a picture of dark woods with an owl and the words *Don't Go*.

Just as my mother had encouraged my father to finish his graduate degree after he was dismissed from the University of North Carolina, she took the lead in helping us heal. She took me to see an educational filmstrip about death at the community college where she had been teaching childbirth classes. As a stoic voice-over played, the cartoon stills told the story of two boys who were off playing in the bushes when one was stung by a bee. The boy was allergic and died, leaving the other to sort out his feelings. I didn't know what to make of the story. On one hand, it left me feeling like I was not alone. But it also left me feeling like I was in a very small and strange club that my mother understood as she sat beside me.

While my dad was more inclined to keep the blinds in Jon's room shut, my mother was the one who opened them first. She put a desk in there, and begun using it as her office: books on childbirth, a demonstration pelvis, a monkey mom doll with a baby and a placenta. Jon's wallpaper remained, along with his posters. On one wall was a peace sign, in red, with Hebrew lettering against a blue background. The words were the hymn *"Hine Ma Tov,"* and the translation ran across the bottom, "Behold How Good and How Pleasant It Is for Brothers to Dwell in Peace." On another wall was Jon's poster of a boy on a white horse by a lake.

One day, six months after Jon's death, she found herself writing on a yellow legal pad. She'd been keeping a diary most her life, dating back to her childhood in Minneapolis, the little brown or red books written in blue cursive. But now she sat at her typewriter with a new kind of urgency: to put down on paper her memories of Jon, to keep them alive. It was as if she couldn't write fast enough, couldn't commit them to paper in time before they vanished like invisible ink.

> I see them returning together. My 3 sons, they're so proud of David. Oh God, let them remember Jon, his sweetness, their brother. It feels good, though, I cry, to write about him, to gather my thoughts and memories together about him. I need to hang on to the memories, the special little things, the everyday feelings we had for him. To forget these things would add to our loss. What do we have but some pictures, the things he made set in his room, our little den now, throughout the house. When will we be able to put up his pictures . . . How many more birthdays (my last one was so painful without him) before I begin to not miss him or think—"he's not here." Will that ever happen? Do I want that to happen? Yet how long can we live—I live—having the pain of it happening?
>
> I want more memories to come to me. I want those who loved him, played with him, got a kick out of him, to write down some memories of him, to add to these.
>
> I see him wiping his finger across his nose. I did that, too. Did he learn that from me? I see him sniffing up, lip slightly down in a sort of habit-like manner. I see his twinkling, twinkling brown yes. I see the little blackhead on his right cheek near his ear. I long for this kid, my Jon, part of me.
>
> I think that my grief might keep me from Andy and

David, lessen my time and commitments to them. That would be so unfair, not right. But my grief separates me from my wholeness now. Maybe time *will* help. More memories: Our stay at the Sandcastle, St. Pete. He and Andy running from pool to pool, enjoying.

Lying in the back of the wagon (on pillows for a while) taking lots of books, comics to read whenever we would drive somewhere. Andy did that, too. Now David does.

The time Gil, Andy, David, Jon, and I rode our bikes (David on mine) to the park, the ducks, the swings.

The time I look out the garage and see Andy's head barely above the Toyota steering wheel with Jon seated next to him driving slowly past the mailbox.

Trying to play the drums, little quick repetitive hits on it. He wanted to take lessons.

Last Yom Kippur. He would get so tired at evening services. He begins to fall asleep, his head leans on my shoulder . . .

His last birthday party, some friends go with him to Shakey's. He liked that a lot. Presents, his own pizza, a Shakey's hat. I hear and see his giggles, he walks fast, his arms swinging, his toes pointed in a little.

Tomorrow is Passover. Last Passover, together here in our new house and Jon here. How many holidays will pass and will his presence not be so missed?

[Our friend's] house, one Sunday last summer. Jon went out on their kayak. He paddles and maneuvered around. He dragged it up on the ground. He was so fervently busy and absorbed.

To remember and see him in all those places. That is what I want now.

And Busch Gardens, see him and Andy dashing up and around to go on the flume ride.

Andy said after Jon's death, "Now I don't have a brother to do things with." He also said, "Did he know I loved him?"

14

Soon I was walking down the same sidewalk where I last saw Jon, and wandering to school alongside the woods where he vanished. Jon was gone but everywhere. He was in the woods across the street from our house. He was in the 7-Eleven that we passed frequently. He was at IDS, in the trees and the Dome. He was in our den, where his last school picture hung next to Andy's and mine against the wood-paneled wall. That picture of him took on great meaning. It was the one that I would see periodically in news stories about his case. My brother wore a red shirt, zipped up to the neck, red like his hair. Red became the color of Jon. Red, the color of his pop art wallpaper. Red like his bike. Red like blood. Red like fire ants. Red was everywhere, and so was my brother. When I was given something of Jon's as a keepsake, it was his lucky rabbit's foot. And it was red too.

It was still the early seventies, and even Jon's murder didn't seem to hamper the sense of freedom that the other kids and I felt at IDS. The nightmare had left us shaken but with an even greater appreciation of what it meant to be alive. This sentiment was written into the school yearbook from 1973. A full page is dedicated to Jon, and shows a black-and-white picture of him against a black background. Jon stands barefoot in front of our house, arms at his side in a white muscle shirt and shorts, head tilted, smiling. The final page of the yearbook shows a photo of a long-haired girl named Betsy, kneeling by IDS's cypress-lined pond, leaning back against her mud-crusted Converse sneakers, hands in her lap, staring up at the sky. The text of a poem that she had written in the wake of Jon's death appears above her. It describes the natural wonders around her and concludes: "Death whispers in my ear; I look once again to see. Life is beautiful."

Life *was* beautiful at IDS. After starting kindergarten there in 1974, I spent my days drifting between the brown circular pods for classes, passing peacocks in my path. A pony-tailed teacher in a flowered skirt taught us how to sauté green beans and onions. We sculpted pottery and fired it in the kiln. A skinny, funny hippie with a long beard taught us how to make whistles from clay. At nap time, we stretched out on thickly woven fringed mats.

Greater freedom awaited us outside on the vast wooded lakeside acreage. There didn't seem to be any limit on how far we could go for recess and lunch. Every tree begged to be climbed. We conquered one tree at a time, and each had its own personality: the fat oak on the main field with the thick gray branches that shot out horizontally, the tall, straight cypress with the rough, scratchy bark. Down by the lake, we pulled ourselves up the melaleuca "paper" tree, a twisting Tolkien-esque giant with a papery bark.

There was a palpable collective energy during free time, a self-organizing tribal urgency that took over my friends and me as we set off on our missions. The moment the door of our pod opened, we'd sprint into the woods, grabbing long sticks and preparing for whatever it was we were to accomplish that day. There were forts to build, treasures to hunt, every knot in every tree a place of hidden fortune.

I fashioned myself as leader of the adventure club. One day I convened my legion to excavate a knothole that, I imagined, housed a giant lost diamond. You could see the diamond down there, I said, if you backed up and stood in the right spot. My friends Michael, Kevin, and Robbie elbowed each other for a look, and claimed they saw it—the glimmer of light reflecting off the crystalline shard. The fact that the glimmer was actually coming from an old sandwich bag didn't faze us; it was a diamond if we said it was.

The explorations didn't come without risk, which made our capers all the more exciting. We could plummet out of trees, eat a rotten kumquat, fall into the lake. But we never heard any mention of words like liability and lawsuit from the teachers; everything was fair game. Most of the danger came in the form of fire ants, nasty little red stingers that burn when they bite. The fire ants were everywhere, scurrying over one another in giant gray mounds of sand that dotted the fields and the bases of trees like camouflaged land mines. Once, I slid down a slide right into a huge pile of ants, much to the delight of my friends. But the teachers kept bottles of calamine lotion on their shelves, and the pasty, cool swabs on my skin made everything okay.

If the teachers were giving me special attention because of Jon's murder, I wasn't aware. No one ever said anything or asked how I was doing, not that I expected them to or even desired this.

They treated me like a bomb they didn't know how to defuse, so they just left me alone. I made it relatively easy for them. Despite what had happened, I was generally a fun-loving and easygoing kid, eager to entertain if not be a bit precocious. Sometimes I'd lash out, throwing a tantrum that the teachers seemed to regard as something to be expressed, not contained. Rather than telling me to stop, they would hand me a hammer and a block of wood and tell me to go get out my anger. So there I would be, standing outside the brown round pod, banging a hammer against the wood until someone told me to come back inside.

Eventually I learned my own coping technique on the schoolyard. It started after kids would come up to me and repeat rumors they had heard about how Jon had been killed. Because I still didn't know the whole story, I had no idea what to believe. Even the most outlandish suggestions could be true. They said he had been cut up and put in a pickle jar, and that he had been shot with bows and arrows. At first, I would just stand there not knowing how to respond. I pictured a boy in a pickle jar, like something out of a *Flat Stanley* children's book, and it didn't make sense.

I took solace telling myself they were wrong. My mind clung to the sparse details that I'd retained: he'd been hit in the head, suffocated, that was that. Everything else was just a lie, some crazy rumors that filled my classmates' heads. Perhaps I actually took the time to respond to them at first, insisting that, no, you're wrong, nothing like that happened to him. But my responses were not convincing enough, because the rumors, as the months went on, kept resurfacing. Finally, I'd had enough, and decided to simply shut down completely in these moments and act like I couldn't hear them.

In that silent space, the world around me would blur and fade—the sounds, the colors, the trees. I was just walking through a thick translucent jelly, isolated, alone. I didn't want pity, my stomach turned at the very thought. To be pitied was to be denigrated; to be singled out as "different." I wanted disregard. I wanted to be just like every other kid around me, seemingly unburdened and intact. I didn't want to be the star of a crime drama; a murder mystery that was fueling all kinds of conversations in the homes of my friends. Every day, on my way to school and back, I would pass the woods where Jon had disappeared. And at some point, a thought occurred to me: perhaps if I hadn't asked Jon for the alligator candy, he would never have gone that day, and he would still be alive.

15

ANDY GREW a giant afro. Even for the midseventies, it was impressive, especially on a white Jewish teenager in the suburbs. The hairdo struck me as an architectural marvel, and I used to watch him tend to it in the mirror of our bathroom. It started out long and wet, but then he'd have at it with his wide black hair pick, flicking and snapping over and over and over again until it dried into a frizzy, dark dome that, if it possessed self-luminescence, would have passed for one of those party lights at Spencer Gifts.

Afros seemed to be everywhere in those days, from Sly Stone and Dr. J to the cast of *Welcome Back, Kotter*. For Andy, the Jewfro was all about the music it conjured, jazz and funk, and his passion for playing the trumpet. Day and night, I'd hear him behind his closed door, practicing scales on his horn. Before long, there were other skinny, white, nerdy funksters in our house, pushing around the living room furniture so they could practice together.

Andy named his band Rhythm and began getting gigs around town. Every weekend, we'd pile into our station wagon and head for Shakey's Pizza Parlor, where Rhythm had a regular show. The station wagon was the perfect roadie vehicle. It was roomy enough to cart the instruments and, for a reason that escaped me, had a mushroom decal by the gas tank. Andy made a point of letting me help the band set up.

As Andy and the band made their way through Dixieland songs, heavyset Southerners—men in trucker hats, women in plaid shirts—would swill their pitchers of beer and hit the dance floor. At some point, Andy would lead a few contests for the kids in the crowd. I went onstage for a balloon-blowing competition, but, shamefully, broke into tears when another kid popped his balloon first.

Shakey's led to Andy's best gig: being the house band at Tampa Stadium, the seventy-two-thousand-seat arena where the Rowdies soccer team played. Soccer was huge at the time, especially in the years before Tampa got a pro football team, and I'd dart between seeing Rodney Marsh play Pelé on the field and seeing Andy play a song by the group Chicago. Andy became just as famous at shul, where he was the designated shofar blower on the high holidays, the yarmulke pinned precariously to his Jewfro as he held the *tekiah gedolah*—the longest note of the service—for what seemed like forever.

Throughout it all, Andy and I seldom, if ever, discussed Jon. We were acclimating from being three brothers to two. He still had a little brother, and I still had a big one. But we knew who was missing in the middle, just like Jon's missing name on the sidewalk in front of our house. But this downsizing became a quiet, personal conundrum for me every time some new person I met asked me how many siblings I had. The question swirled inside my head for years: Should I say one or two brothers? Should I say I *had* two brothers but now I have one?

If I say "one," then that erases Jon's existence, as if he never had been here. And saying "one" raised questions. People wondered why Andy and I were so far apart in age: eight and half years. It seemed suspicious. Some asked if I was a mistake. But even that was better than having to tell them the truth that I still didn't fully understand: I had two brothers but one was dead.

"How'd he die?"

He was killed.

"How?"

He was murdered.

"How? Why? What happened?"

And so on. The questions were too much for me to deal with, so I decided it was better not to deal with them at all. "I have one brother," I'd say, even though it felt like a lie.

Given our disparity in ages, it was hard, as a child, to know what Andy was struggling with at the time. Though we didn't talk about this, we felt it. We shared a sense of unspoken fraternity, an incredible love and closeness, like two guys who'd returned from the front lines of some invisible war. Though Jon's absence wasn't articulated, I felt it every time I walked down toward Andy's room at the end of the hall. He'd be in there with the door locked, listening to music on his headphones or playing drums. As I knocked persistently at the door, I'd cast a glance to my right into Jon's old bedroom. Though my mom was using it as her office, I could still feel Jon's presence there.

All else that was left of Jon's were a few items that he had saved in a small brown wooden box in his closet. In private moments, I would stand on a chair and pull the box from the shelf, unlocking the gold clasp and slowly opening it. The box smelled nutty and musty. Inside was a small black plastic water pistol, a few dollar bills, a spool of caps for a cap gun, and an audiotape that Jon had made with his friend.

One day I finally got the nerve to put the tape into the cassette deck and press Play. I sat on the carpet, listening and watching the tape spin, recalling the days I'd spend there with him playing with the flight book. The two black capstans spun the tape along, as I waited with anticipation. Then I heard the hiss of the tape, and the sound of a voice: "Oh yeah," it said. The voice was high pitched, almost girly, perhaps made when he was much younger. The voice sang some incomprehensible words, then said "bye." Then came a click and some hiss, and another voice: now a boy's voice affecting the deep tones of an adult. "Hello, this is Howard Cosell down in New York City," Jon said, "and Underdog has just been fatally hurt."

Underdog was our favorite cartoon. It chronicled the adventures of an ordinary pooch with a secret superpower identity, Underdog. He would fight battles against the villainous Simon Bar Sinister, an evil doctor with a greenish head shaped like a decaying tooth. His girlfriend was the comely canine reporter, Sweet Polly Purebread. Jon was enacting his own episode in which Underdog finds trouble and gets interviewed by the famous sportscaster. He went on as the voice of Cosell. "May I have a word with you, Underdog?" he asked the wounded hero.

"Ugh," Jon replied as Underdog.

Then he slipped back into his announcer's voice. "This is Howard Cosell going to Sweet Polly Purebread."

"Hey," Jon said in Polly's squeaky voice, "this is Sweet Polly Purebread, and Underdog has just been killed. Oh yeah yeah yeah. And Simon Bar Sinister has just conquered the world." Then Jon's voice vanished and was replaced by an electromagnetic hiss.

16

DAD TALKED with the chimps. It was the highlight of our trips to Busch Gardens, the Africa-themed amusement park near our house. The chimpanzees inhabited a large, open play area around the middle of the park. They lazed on giant fake boulders and swung from tire swings. My dad would step up to the rock wall surrounding the chimps and open his mouth wide, baring his teeth and widening his eyes. The chimps wouldn't pay attention at first. But then, after hearing his convincing clicking sounds, one or two would casually take notice.

As my dad twisted his face and mouth, the chimps actually began to mimic and respond to his gestures—cackling and gaping as if they were conversing with a bushy faced uncle. Jolly tourists in matching T-shirts and hats would also take notice, wandering over with their fried lunch to watch the man with long black hair and black beard chattering with the chimps. They assumed my dad was an employee of Busch Gardens—some monkey expert putting on an afternoon show. I knew better, that my dad was drawing from his anthropological expertise to have a little fun and entertain his kid.

I wasn't aware, not consciously anyway, of how Jon's death was affecting my mom and dad. As much as they may have discussed grief and suffering with each other and with their peers, we didn't talk about Jon much with one another. Or at least he wasn't being discussed very often with me. I sensed that even uttering Jon's name was too painful between us, too real, too raw. There was one time when my mom and I were discussing Jon, and I watched as my dad quietly stood up and left the room. I didn't feel rejected or hurt, I just felt curious and confused, struggling to understand what was going through his head. The word *murdered* was never mentioned. If anything, we would use the word *died*, as if not mentioning the *M*-word would somehow make it less difficult.

I had no idea how Jon's murder had transformed the way my father parented me. My dad had been through a sort of mirror experience of loss and suffering, losing his father when he was nine, and then losing his eleven-year-old son when he was a father. I didn't know what regrets he harbored, what guilt he carried. I had no idea how he had spent most of his years as a father before I was born, working long hours as a rising professor, studying and writing while his sons Jon and Andy grew. I knew they'd had their special times together, hiking through the mountains and foothills of Tucson. But I didn't realize how one way he coped with Jon's death was by making up for lost time with me.

Busch Gardens was a big part of this. Though we didn't have a lot of money, he got season passes for us, and we went almost every weekend. Sometimes we'd spend a long day there, riding the flume and eating pretzels while tourists waited in long lines for free Busch beer at the Hospitality House. Other times we'd just go to ride the Skyride, my favorite attraction, which would carry us along quietly in a cart high above the park, and then come home. We also started going to watch sports, getting season tickets for the Rowdies and the Tampa Bay Buccaneers, who'd entered the National Football League in 1976. Or we'd go off to the schoolyard to fly a kite, or toss the football around in the back. My dad, like my mom, lived passionately and with great humor. He gave big hugs and loved eating, danced as Tevye in a synagogue production of *Fiddler on the Roof.* He always had the capacity to feel and express tremendous joy.

The headaches, though, were still striking him at random. Once, we were at a showing of *Clash of the Titans* when I heard his measured breathing and saw his face droop down, tears rolling from his eyes. When he said we had to go, I understood.

My dad's master's program in applied anthropology had begun in full force in the fall of 1974, less than a year after Jon's death, and, as the department chair, it kept him busy in the months to come. For me, trips to the Anthropology Department were the ultimate adventure. I saw halls full of people with long hair and jeans like my dad, passionate, intelligent grown-ups with great senses of humor. Dad's office door was covered in newspaper clippings and cartoons, including *Doonesbury* and R. Crumb comics. The room was thick with cigarette smoke, as students came and went.

Down the hall was the physical anthropology lab, a wonderland of bones and skulls. The fact that they were human bones and skulls didn't strike me as weird. I just knew that Kurt, the professor who ran the place, was always happy to let me check out the jawbones and teeth. On special days, I got to go along on the archaeology digs in the woods, using a giant sifter to search for fossils. Whenever my IDS class took a field trip to my dad's department, I was always proud to show off the pictures of him in the small museum doing fieldwork in Israel. Anthropologists began filling our house again for the frequent office parties, which soon resumed at my home. Once again I was back in my favorite environment, sprinting over the thick yellow shag carpet through the forest of legs as jazz records played.

On weekends my father would sometimes accompany me to synagogue, where I was enrolled in Hebrew school. The shul teemed with big Southern Jews, men in pale blue suits and colorful yarmulkes kibbitzing over coffee served in white plastic cups, bosomy women tending to the grits, the eggs, and the kids. We darted between them, heading full speed for the pastries, the black-and-white cookies, the gooey rugelach. But there were obstacles, particularly the old ladies in their synagogue best, slightly hunched, wearing white lace coverings on their heads. The old Jewish ladies were tough, shuffling along the dessert table with a napkin spread out expertly in their palms, as they filled their hands with goodies and then shoved the bounty stealthily into their perfumed handbags.

The running inevitably stopped when we were corralled into services. We'd sit there on the brown, cushy fold-down seats, holding the prayer book in our hands as the cantor sang the familiar Hebrew prayers, sometimes blowing on a little pitch pipe first. The services had a rhythm and a cadence all their own. The melodies seemed to build and beautify as they reached the end of the service—perhaps because the end meant the sooner I could climb back into the station wagon and go home to watch *Creature Feature*, a weekly matinee of monster movies, on TV while eating leftover roast chicken.

During the service, I didn't understand what was being said or how I might extrapolate meaning for my own life. The Hebrew was beyond me, and the English translation always seemed to be essentially the same: praising the Lord over and over. Instead, I would tunnel into my imagination, the skill I'd been building at IDS, and it served me well here. Sometimes I would bring props to help me, such as broken magnets I could stealthily assemble into a magnet monster, or a watch with a Twist-O-Flex band that I could maneuver in exponential variations.

But while I would be off in my own world during Saturday school services, I felt differently when my dad came along. There was a comfort in his presence, the familiarity of his voice singing the hymns, the way he harmonized—just like he harmonized when he sang Pete Seeger songs at home. As he sang, sitting next to me, I would play with the ends of his tallith, his prayer shawl, twisting the white fringes between my small fingers. Occasionally my dad would take notice, and rather than admonishing me, he'd slip the tallit from my hand and playfully tickle my nose and eyelashes with the fringes, which always made me smile.

But then the point would come in the service for the mourner's Kaddish, the prayer said by those over thirteen who had recently lost a loved one or on the anniversary of a death. As was customary, the mourners would rise while everyone else remained seated. When our family said Kaddish, I would notice the eyes of the congregants looking back at us, perhaps only for a moment before they turned away. Some people in the synagogue didn't like the idea of standing during the Kaddish because it made them feel awkward. But my dad said that standing was the point; you stood so that other people in the shul could know that you were grieving and show their support.

As I listened to my parents say the prayer—"*Yit'gadal v'yit'kadash sh'mei raba . . .*"—I knew that they were saying the words for Jon, and that Jon was on the minds of everyone who saw them standing there. We were a public family, and Jon's murder was a part of the community. This wasn't the same for the other deaths, I realized. No one knew the story of my dad's father, Abraham, when my dad said Kaddish for him. But when my family stood for Jon, they saw the emptiness that was there, the missing person in our family who never returned.

I didn't imagine how Jon's death must have impacted every other parent in that place, how they must have held their own children close, thankful that they didn't have to endure such pain or wonder how they could possibly survive if they ever did. Instead, I just saw the way they glanced away from us, or how, on our way out, someone might hug my parents or take their hands gently.

In those moments, I knew that this death transcended my own family in a way that was beyond my comprehension. Part of me felt exposed and vulnerable by this attention, but another part of me felt supported and nurtured. Even though my childhood amnesia left me without the details of Jon's murder, during the week that he was missing, and the aftermath, I could see that the adults around me carried the memories with them. They had been there with my parents, although doing what I didn't know. They had seen things, learned things, understood something that perhaps I would too one day.

17

My mother would see Jon occasionally in her dreams. One came in late April 1975. In the dream, he looked as he did about a year before his death: shorter hair, uneasy from struggling at school. He was away at a camp—one from which he was never returning. But he was able to write home every few days. Each of us received a thick letter folded into a tiny envelope. The letter to my dad told him that everything was okay where Jon was now. When my mother awoke, she began writing on her legal pad in her office, his old room, to get it down before she forgot.

The dreams made her feel all the more resolved to do what she could to preserve his memory. "I don't believe in life after death," she wrote. "I only believe *we* give a person immortality and do so by remembering, thinking about, bringing to mind, touching, smelling, sensing in our heads all the details about the dead one we love. Maybe our concern for our mortality made us discover how to capture an image in a photograph. The special pain of looking hard and long at the picture. I have tapes of Jon. I'm afraid to listen to them. Why? Why not? What can be more painful, the cloudlike transparent memory of his voice and image, or the absolute almost solid image of his recorded voice, like a photograph."

And yet, she realized, her pain was changing, internalizing in ways she was trying to understand. "I haven't cried for Jon for a while," she wrote. "Pain without tears (like I used to have). Maybe it's because the grief has taken root. While rooting, the aura of new grief bubbles and rises almost constantly to the surface. But it's deep and rooted and solidly planted and the motions and responses are firm and rooted and always a part of our very soul. *Never* will I cease to love this Jon, or stop longing for him. We must remember him, talk about him, bring his image and sounds to our consciousness."

While we were now all back in our routines—me at school, Andy at school and playing in his band, my dad at the university, my mom teaching Lamaze—we were each still in our own private orbit. But it was my mother, once again, who took the lead, just as she had been the one to open the door to Jon's room again. She wanted to reach out, to talk with someone else who could understand and share her pain. "Bring me a mother," she told my dad one day.

The president of the university had lost a child as well, and his wife agreed to meet with my mother. Though the woman had lost her child to illness, there was a comfort between them, a motherly understanding of what it felt like to bear a child and lose the child too young. It felt like such a taboo at the time to talk about death so openly, and yet it provided so much solace. They resolved to bring in other parents who had lost children too.

At the time in the midseventies, the field of death and dying, which echoed the name of Elizabeth Kübler-Ross's pioneering

1969 book, was still new. The movement challenged what one practitioner called our "death-denying culture" by probing and plumbing the universal question: how to cope with the end of life, both our own and others. But for my mother, the death and dying movement seemed like a natural extension of the social action she and my father had taken part in over their lives. The denial of death had created a kind of mass oppression, a culture of silence that left mourners feeling alienated and ill-equipped. Grievers were supposed to buck up, be "strong," not cry in public, or carry on about their suffering beyond an acceptable period of time. By exploring the experience of loss, the death and dying movement was giving voice to the voiceless.

Once again, a personal experience—Jon's death—had drawn my parents into social action, just as my mother sought Lamaze before Andy's birth and my father sang union songs as a young activist in the Bronx. They had come to D&D, as they nicknamed it, to help them survive the seemingly unsurvivable, and part of helping themselves was to establish this community for others.

After leading informal support groups, my parents started one of the country's first chapters of Compassionate Friends, a support group that had begun in England for parents' who'd lost children. It felt radical at the time—gathering others like themselves to share their losses, their struggles—as radical as fighting to let fathers in the delivery room or staging sit-ins at lunch counters during the civil rights era. My father, though he had been suffering largely in silence, followed my mom's lead, and the two poured their hearts into the movement. They organized conferences and helped launch the area's first hospice. My dad began a long correspondence with Holocaust survivor and author Elie Wiesel.

From my vantage point, the D&D (a phrase I later equated with the role-playing game Dungeons & Dragons) crowd resembled the same kind of people I'd seen around my house for years: long-haired men and women in faded jeans and silver jewelry. And they seemed just as passionate and full of life, surrounded by music and food and laughter. But then I'd notice something else occasionally pass across their faces: expressions of seriousness and gravity that I had become accustomed to seeing when people approached my parents or Andy and me.

At one point, my parents introduced me to an older man with a long gray ponytail and kind eyes. His name was John Brantner, and he had become a close friend of theirs. A psychologist from Minnesota, Brantner spoke of such things as "positive approaches to dying," the title of one lecture. "Could we start at the end of a relationship instead of the beginning and work our way backward—see what the ending means to it?" He said in that presentation, "Could we use grief in a positive way to inform our other relationships, our ongoing relationships, and relationships that are yet to come?"

The pain of loss had another side, he said, speaking of how suffering could make a person "splendid"—more able to appreciate the range of human existence and emotions. He said that if he could wish one thing for a child, it would be that the child live through a death or a divorce so as to gain the wisdom that came with such experiences. But, he went on, the child must go through these experiences with at least one supportive person. More than anything, Brantner empathized with my family. When my parents met with him, my mother told him, "I can't drive behind a car and see a trunk without thinking of Jonathan in the trunk."

"Now I'll think about that too," he replied.

"That was to me one of the most profound therapeutic things at the time: empathy," my mother later recalled. "Another thing he said to me that was really scary was you can't be assured this won't happen again," she said, "I thought, *Oh God, how can I go through that again*? He said, 'It's the people, it's the support, it's the community.' "

This growing sense of community became manifest on May 16, 1975. An Israeli artist and family friend, Kopel Gurwin, had been commissioned to create two banners that would hang in our synagogue in Jon's memory. There was one on either side of the entrance lobby. On the right hung a banner in blues and greens, showing a cluster of animals around a child, inside a mosaic of shapes. On the border were Hebrew words, the last clause from a biblical passage "[A] child shall lead them." It translated to: "And the wolf shall dwell with the lamb, and the leopard shall lie down with the kid; And the calf and the young lion and the fatling together; And a little child shall lead them." A plaque alongside the banner noted that in this banner, "Gurwin seeks to capture Isaiah's messianic vision of a world at harmony, enjoying peace, relationship and love . . . The figure of a child, secure and unafraid, leads the world to better understanding of harmony."

On the left hung a banner called *Jonathan's Covenant*. It showed two cubist figures, in purples and reds, with faces pressed side by side, and was taken from a biblical passage about two characters who happened to share my and Jonathan's names. "The banner depicts the strong filial love shared between Jonathan and David," the plaque to the banners read, and "suggests the loving relationship shared by Jonathan Kushner and his brothers."

I had no idea what passage it referred to; it just struck me as strange that there were two friends in the Bible with the same names as us. I also felt a bit guilty that there wasn't an Andy up there too, although I knew that this was not intentional; it was just part of the Bible story. Alongside the border were Hebrew words that were translated on the plaque: ". . . and the Lord be with thee, as He hath been with my father . . . and Jonathan caused David to swear again by the love that he had for him: for he loved him as he loved his own soul."

18

AT SOME POINT, I saw their faces. The older one had short, dark hair and a high forehead, buggy eyes, a thick mustache. The newspaper photo of the younger one showed him with his eyes shut, thick hair swept low over his right eye; he wore a dark T-shirt. As far as I could recall, no one sat me down and showed me the pictures of the men who murdered my brother. I would just occasionally see the photos in a newspaper left on the kitchen table alongside the comics, the sports, the weather. Apparently something was happening—something in the court system—that was keeping the story in the news, even years later.

I could bear to look at the pictures only for so long before I had to turn away. Part of me wanted to know more about these men: Who were they? What exactly did they do? They knew the answers to everything that haunted me. How long had they been in those woods? How long had they planned this? Was there a reason they selected him?

But the part of me that wanted to know all this was small. The rest of me felt sickened, frightened, horrified that there were actually real people behind my brother's death. Before seeing their faces, I had consoled myself by keeping their images in the abstract; by not visualizing anyone at all. All I saw was my own edited filmstrip of Jon's final day: our conversation, his departure, the blur of the red metal bike, the banana seat, the high handlebars, twirling pedals, the woods, and then a curtain of darkness dropping forever. I didn't want to see the faces that were watching Jon that day. I certainly didn't want to know their names. All I caught was the last name of the older one, Witt, and the moment I saw it, I tried to erase it from my mind.

Though I was just a child, the older I became, the more my mind struggled with the looming mystery of Jon's murder. Of course, in one sense, there was no mystery at all. The facts were out there somewhere. The case, as far as I knew, had been solved. But because the facts were beyond me—beyond my courage or ability to ask the questions that would reveal them—the mystery festered and grew. The most mysterious thing of all to me was how something like this could happen in the first place. And, more terrifyingly, if this could happen to Jon, then—and this fear could not be assuaged—it could happen to someone else: my friends, my family, me.

Kids grow up hearing fairy tales, but the biggest fairy tale of all, I realized at the age of four, is that life is safe. Life isn't safe, I learned. It's crazy. Evil is real. One minute you could be riding your bike on the way to get candy, and the next, you're dead. Anything could happen anywhere at any time. So now what? How was I supposed to live without giving in to the fear? Every kid fears the bogeyman, the creature in the closet, the monster under the bed. But my bogeyman had a face—two faces—and they couldn't be dispelled by someone telling me he wasn't real.

Unfortunately, I was an imaginative kid, and the less I knew, the more terrible things I invented in my mind. With so many holes in the central story of my life in tatters, I filled in the blanks myself, like scribbling in a giant Mad Lib.

"My brother Jon was biking through the woods when a man hit him with a ________ NOUN and then gagged him with a ________ NOUN. Then they ________ VERB to the ________ NOUN. It took Jon ________ NUMBER ________ UNITS OF TIME to die. The reason he was missing for a week was because they ________ VERB him and then they took him to the ________ NOUN and then . . ."

From there the story degenerated into dark fantasy. It felt like I was in bed, holding that magical old edition of *Grimm's Fairy Tales* that was coming to life. The letters fell from the pages, which became windows to some other world. Each page I flipped had the same image: a scene of a dark forest. The faster I turned the pages, the quicker the scene came to life: a sticky black ooze on the floor of the woods rising up to the tops of the trees until the ooze was coming out of the floor of my room, up through my blue shag carpet, past the orange plastic night table, up alongside my bed, spilling over my fuzzy orange blanket, up the walls of the playing-card-soldier wallpaper, past the blue strips of the Venetian blinds, up toward the ceiling that I had tacked with football pennants—the blackness was everywhere. In those dark moments, I felt immobilized both by what I knew and by what I didn't know, and I was drowning.

By 1980 the awful reality of child murder became impossible to push away. It seeped into my house through the portal of my television. I'd be sitting on the couch in our den, waiting for a new episode of *M*A*S*H* or *The Jeffersons*, when there'd be another newsbreak—another grainy video of adults searching a forest, or police officers carrying a stretcher with a small mound wrapped on top. The "Atlanta Child Murders," as they were known, had become a nationwide saga. Day after day, newscasts carried the stories of the missing African-American boys and unsolved murders.

Sometimes my mom or dad would be sitting next to me when the reports came on, and I would feel an icy stillness envelop us. Nothing was said, and nothing had to be said. I knew that we were all flashing to Jon, to the woods, to our story. And I desperately wanted the moment to pass, the report to end, and to have George Jefferson or Hawkeye Pierce bound back across the screen. My eyes would leave the TV and travel over the wood paneling, past the burbling fish tank, the bookshelves of Tom Robbins and Elie Wiesel novels, and up the wall to the gold-framed photo of Jon: the one that had been used on all the missing person fliers, the one that still ran in the papers whenever the case resurfaced, the one of him in the red shirt, head tilted, smiling.

But it was getting harder to wish away the news of missing kids on TV. Something seemed to be changing in America. Stories of missing kids were in the headlines more frequently. It had started the year before, on May 25, 1979, when a six-year-old boy in Manhattan, Etan Patz, vanished on the morning of his first solo walk to his school bus, just two blocks away from home. While abductions had been relegated to local news in the past, the unique nature of the Patz story—the SoHo location, the first trip to school—riveted the New York tabloids and spread nationwide.

The case sparked the missing children movement. The public became aware just how badly coordinated federal, state, and local officials were in sharing information on missing kids. Patz became the first missing child to have his picture appear on milk cartons. Eventually President Ronald Reagan declared May 25, the date of Patz's disappearance, as National Missing Children's Day. The ominous tagline of late-night TV news casts—"It's ten o'clock. Do you know where your children are?"—seemed to take on a new urgency.

With the Patz case unsolved, and the body count in Atlanta racking up to nearly two dozen missing children, a new fear began entering the minds of parents around the country. News reports spoke of curfews in Atlanta and kids feeling more afraid of playing outside. The media seemed to have found a new fear to exploit; every parent's Ultimate Nightmare.

I could see some of the ripple effects of all this reaching Tampa. The story appeared in the local papers and entered conversations among the neighborhood parents. Occasionally I would see them cast a long glance in my direction, perhaps careful not to upset me or maybe to see how I was responding. I gave them no indication of anything. I just went on playing electronic football or Atari, pretending as though I weren't aware, hoping that the attention would go away.

Now and then, though, I would reach out in my own passive-aggressive way. During one community class trip at IDS, we were taken to a local cemetery. While the teacher showed us the different kinds of headstones and crypts, I wandered off by myself and sat by a tree. In a way, it felt so transparent—such a maudlin bid for attention. I remember thinking how badly I wanted the teacher to come over and ask me if I was okay. But I felt too embarrassed and ashamed to ask for comfort myself. Instead, I just sat there for what seemed like forever, picking at blades of grass until the class moved on to another section of the cemetery, and I rejoined them.

Despite the growing awareness of missing kids, we still seemed to have as much freedom as ever. If parents in our town were feeling more afraid, they weren't changing their behavior yet. Kids still went off into the woods behind the 7-Eleven and disappeared on their bikes for hours on end. Even I was able to continue my explorations around the neighborhood. But my parents had limits.

At the peak of the Atlanta murder mystery, IDS organized an Outward Bound trip, one of those adventure excursions that were supposed to teach us confidence through survival skills. After weeks of training, we would then pass the final test. Each kid would have to go off into the woods and spend the night alone. Everyone in my class was going, but the thought of me off in the wilderness by myself was too much for my parents. When my mother and father said they didn't want me to go, I felt disappointed, but I was also relieved.

On June 21, 1981, the Atlanta mystery finally came to an end when police arrested twenty-three-year-old Wayne Williams, who was found guilty of two of the twenty-nine murders and sentenced to life in prison (the murders stopped after he was apprehended). But the new fear didn't end. The next month, six-year-old Adam Walsh was reported missing from a Sears department store in

Hollywood, Florida, where he was playing video games while his mother shopped for a lamp a few aisles away.

Coming on the heels of the Atlanta case, the Walsh murder became another nationwide saga, as police and locals searched in vain for the boy. His severed head was finally found in a canal a few weeks later, but the murderer remained at large. The boy's father, John Walsh, would go on to become an outspoken advocate for missing children. He also founded a nonprofit to fight for improved legislation: the Adam Walsh Outreach Center for Missing Children, which later merged with a newer organization, the National Center for Missing and Exploited Children.

The two-year period between Patz's disappearance and Walsh's murder would prove to be a national tipping point. In 1982 Congress passed the Missing Children's Act to fill the need for a coordinated center of information when a kid disappears. Such resources didn't exist when Jon vanished. The Missing Children's Act empowered the FBI to maintain a database on missing persons that parents and cops around the country could access.

These developments were all beyond me at the time. And I suppose, like everyone else, I went back to my life and pursued my freedom with as much denial as I could muster—just as I had been living for years without truly knowing what had happened to Jon. It was still a mystery to me. A boy a few hours' away in Florida had vanished and been decapitated after he went off to play video games at the mall. But that wasn't going to stop me from disappearing too.

On my eleventh birthday, I asked for a green Schwinn bike that I had seen in the shop. I don't recall being aware or not that this was the same color and make of Jon's last bike, the one he got on his eleventh birthday, or if my parents picked up on the connection. But once I got it I was ready to ride as far away as I could. I had first felt the possibilities of this freedom and adventure when, some years before, my dad taught me how to ride. I was nervous about falling down, but not, as I would recall later, nervous about what it meant for me to be able to ride off on my bike alone. I just wanted mobility, the freedom to go off, to discover, to ride to my friends' houses on my own and feel a sense of independence and power. If I was afraid of what might happen to me—that I might suffer the same fate as my brother—that fear wasn't strong enough to stop me.

As my dad stood by me on my Huffy dirt bike, it clearly wasn't stopping him either. And if he was struggling with this, he didn't let on, not then or later. Instead, he just ran beside me as I wobbled on the bike, steadying me with his hands if I leaned too far. At one point, he couldn't steady me enough, and I flopped over on my side onto the grass. I was fine, and I think we laughed about it. And then I got back on again. It took awhile for me to get my footing, to give myself over to the motion and balance until I wasn't thinking about them anymore. I was just pedaling, fast and furious, as the sound of my father's running feet faded behind me. "How far could I go?" I asked my parents after I learned to ride. "Anywhere but the woods," they said.

19

One would think that my parents, especially, would be the first to keep Andy and me under lock and key, but I experienced almost the opposite and rarely felt anything but freedom. For my parents, it was a constant struggle between what my mother told me later was "the fear and the freedom." She said, "You don't want your kid to be crippled. You want them to be alive and enjoy life. And despite my fears, I couldn't be responsible for keeping you back from enjoying life. But at the same time, I had to be careful."

They weren't able to let my brother and me go right away, but it happened gradually. When I reminded my mother how I used to take off on my bike for hours at a time—and this was long before the age of cell phones—she marveled at it herself. "If I didn't know where you were, if we did that, I don't know how we did it," she said. "But apparently we did."

It wasn't easy. My mother worried, especially at first. Even when they found the courage to let me go, the fear didn't subside. "If you were away and I didn't hear from you, I'd think, *Why didn't he call? Where is he?*" my mother recalled. "I remember so many times when I didn't hear from you and you didn't let me know, I'd get to imagining, *Oh my God, this is so terrible; I'm so frightened of these terrible feelings.*"

And so my parents would reassure each other, and they would find reassurance from friends. As I got older and began staying out late on weekends, a friend suggested to my mother that they have me knock on their bedroom door when I returned, which helped them sleep at night. And when that didn't work, she would simply talk herself down and say, "Wait, they'll come back, they'll be okay."

For Andy, my parents' ability to let go and encourage us to get the most out of life was infectious. Times were not always rosy—there were the usual conflicts between parents and kids—but there was a sense that life was full of wonderful possibilities, despite the horrors. There was so much joy around our house, so many good times; our parents were known for their warmth, their humor, their compassion. He felt even more determined to find the career and life that would fulfill him.

I began spending more and more time out on my bike. I would ride off down the sidewalk alone. Nothing but the pedals under my soles, and the playing card lodged in my back tire spokes simulating motorcycle sounds. I don't remember declaring a destination when I would head off. It was usually just a matter of saying something like, "I'm going to ride my bike," and then hearing my mom mutter something, and then I was off: down the driveway, around the corner, looping down our street, passing the tall palms, friends' houses, maybe pulling in and ringing a doorbell—Is Marty home to play Atari with me?—and either taking a friend with me wherever or just continuing alone on my way.

Out of our street, I'd pick up the sidewalk again along the main road, glancing over my shoulder at the woods where Jon vanished. Disappearing on our bikes didn't just give us more freedom. It gave us the opportunity to fuck up. Fucking up, if no one got hurt, was a good thing. It made me feel alive, urgent. The more I feared the consequences of my mistakes, the less I thought about the absence of Jon. When you fucked up, you discovered yourself more, slammed into the barrier between right and wrong. Before that, you were just pushing in a million directions, pushing in the darkness until you felt a wall. When you pushed so hard that a wall fell down, you knew you'd found one. But you couldn't find one unless you were out in the black.

The first fuckup happened not far from my house, just across the street from the woods that claimed my brother. Lizard Man (a skinny kid who collected lizards), Metal Mouth (a hulking, metal-mouthed kid from Texas), and I were crouching behind a bush with handfuls of kumquats. The fruit, which grew on a tree by a neighbor's house, tasted awfully sour but made for awesome projectiles. They were just small and hard enough to gain speed when you chucked them, but pulpy enough inside to leave a nice sticky splatter.

We were leaving plenty of *splats* as we chucked the kumquats at the cars speeding down the road. One by one, we took turns chucking the little orange fruits at the passing rides, the muscle cars, the pickups, the occasional Mercedes. Once in a while, a car might slow down in response, but we were adept at grabbing our bikes and peeling off unscathed. After I hurled one kumquat at a little sports car, we heard the wheels screech, and we took off as usual for the bikes. But halfway down the block, I checked over my shoulders to see that I was alone.

Lizard Man and Metal Mouth hadn't made it to their bikes, I realized. Instead, they were being screamed at by a giant man who, on closer inspection, appeared to be the quarterback of the Tampa Bay Buccaneers. "Holy shit, it was Doug Williams!" Lizard Man shouted as they finally caught up with me. "You hit Doug Williams's car!" I felt filled with regret, both for getting busted and for missing out on the opportunity to meet Doug Williams in person.

A more serious fuckup came soon after when Lizard Man, Metal Mouth, and I hurled smoke bombs into the creek behind my house. Fireworks had become a passion, both for the pyrotechnics and the illicit nature of the stuff. They were illegal in Florida, and we got them only when someone brought them down from South Carolina. Metal Mouth was a reliable supplier: bottle rockets, M-80s, black snakes, Roman candles, and so on. Smoke bombs I could score myself. Some old ladies somehow got away with selling them in a gift shop in Tarpon Springs, the Greek fishing village outside town.

The smoke bombs were about the size of the kumquats, but came in different colors: red, green, blue, yellow. We lit the end of the short fuse and then chucked the little sizzling balls, waiting for the sulfuric gush of smoke to come out. Metal Mouth, Lizard Man, and I fired our balls into the creek, and delighted in the gust of smoke filling the air. What we didn't anticipate was the giant flame that suddenly licked the sky. Then another flame. And another. Something had caught fire in the creek, and I ran.

I ran until I couldn't run anymore, and didn't even care or turn around to see what had happened to my friends. Later that night I got a call from Lizard Man asking me where I had gone and why I hadn't stuck around to help them put out the flame. Someone had called the fire department, which took care of the blaze before it got out of hand. But we never got blamed or caught. I was starting to get more accustomed to this feeling that came with my increased freedom: guilt. Guilt for fucking up and guilt, I suppose, for being free and alive in the first place. Jon wasn't free. He was dead. And he was dead, I still felt in my dark private moments, because he had gone to get candy for me.

I couldn't take it anymore, the guilt, the not knowing. I had grown up not talking about Jon's murder, walking away in silence whenever the subject came up, but the fears and feelings, the mystery and madness, it was all still there and triggered easily. This happened once in ninth grade at Tampa Prep, the private school I was attending on the campus of the University of Tampa. After school, I'd hang out with my friends Vince and Doug, brothers who shared my affinity for comics and the group Rush. After school, we'd debate the merits of the first side of Rush's album *Hemispheres* versus side one of *2112* while heading off downtown, walking past the homeless guys and hookers, making our way to the Greek sandwich shop with the Galaga arcade machine. We didn't have to tell anyone where we were going or leave a note—we would just go.

One of those days, though, I couldn't go with them. I had to get back home for some reason. But the next morning, they told me, with flushed faces and excited voices, that I should have come along. "We found a dead body," Doug said. They had been wandering around campus, when they strolled into a warehouse for the hell of it. That's when they saw her: a dead woman, decomposing in a pile of garbage in the back. Next thing they knew, the cops were there, and they were giving statements, but they didn't know what happened to her, and probably never would.

I could see Doug's and Vince's faces change as they recalled their discovery, the mix of fascination and repulsion, but the one thing I didn't see was the emotion I was feeling at that moment: fear. All I could think about was how easily I might have been with them, and how I might have stumbled on the body, and how awful that would feel, how scared I'd be, how I'd think that maybe that she was killed, and if she was killed, who killed her, and where were they, and were they there now, and could they be coming for us—for me. Fear shot through me in a way I couldn't control or understand. I had no idea what post-traumatic stress disorder was, or that I was surely suffering from it. And the fact that I was feeling this fear at all, even though I was standing safely in the hallway outside my ninth-grade English class, didn't matter. Everything they were telling me was just hitting way too close to home, and the fact that they didn't seem to know my backstory—or perhaps didn't let on—only made me feel more isolated.

I still didn't have the will or nerve to grill my parents on the details of Jon's death. I was close with Andy, but he was now off at college, and I rarely saw him outside of the occasional holiday. I let it all pass. Maybe I was still just protecting them, hesitant to ask them to relive such a dark chapter of their lives. Or maybe I just couldn't deal with acknowledging the reality of Jon's murder with my parents—that somehow, by not discussing his death, we could survive more easily. But I was growing up. I needed answers. And I knew where to find them.

20

"WHERE CAN I see the *Tampa Tribune* from October 1973?"

When I asked this question of the librarian, I probably seemed like any other thirteen-year-old researching a report. During lunch at school, I wandered into the library of the nearby University of Tampa one day. But I felt like I was transparent, as if just uttering the request, particularly the date, was some dead giveaway to her. After spending so many years at IDS, where everyone knew our family's story, I couldn't shake the feeling that the story had followed me everywhere, like a sign taped by a bully to my back.

Of course, the librarian had no clue why I was there, as she handed me the small blue box of microfilm. It seemed remarkably light for something so heavy. I had never read the newspaper reports about my brother's death, beyond catching the occasional headline when a story was left on the kitchen table. Part of me didn't want to spool the reel through the microfilm reader, didn't want to know what I didn't know, didn't want to learn what I hadn't learned. But there seemed to be an inevitability to the moment, some fated flow of movement, a lifting of the arms, a maneuvering of the microfilm, a squinting of the eyes as the projector lamp shone through the membrane, as my thumb and forefinger adjusted a knob, and the past snapped into focus on-screen. I felt like a Hardy Boy amateur detective searching for clues to a murder mystery.

With a twist of the knob, the microfilm began to blur by in black horizontal streaks, like the threaded clouds of an approaching storm. Periodically I would release the knob, let the film come to a halt, check the date with anticipation and dread, and then resume the inky rush. The closer I got to October, the slower I turned the spool, and the more discernible the newspaper copy began to be. I saw headlines about Watergate, the unbeaten Vikings, the movie *Shaft*. I passed ads for discount tires and boxy televisions and banana-seat bicycles. It seemed so long ago, another era, another world—not even my own, really—but the one I remembered only in glimpses. The days of getting up from the couch to flip the channel on the TV, the banana-seat bike of Jon's, the mushroom decal on the back of our station wagon.

At first I stopped at October 28, the day Jon was killed, scanning the headlines for a few moments until I realized that, of course, there would be no news of him that day. No one knew what had happened yet or that he was missing. The news, I suspected, would start the next day, October 29, and it did: "*In Woods*," read the headline, "Hunt Is On for Boy, 11, Feared Lost."

"A massive search party of some 150 firemen, police and residents was formed last night to comb a wooded area north of Carrollwood where an 11-year-old boy is believed to have disappeared," the story began. "Hillsborough County's sheriff officials said the boy, Jonathan Kushner . . . was last seen around noon yesterday near a 7-Eleven store . . . The search for the youth 'officially' began after 6 p.m., deputies said, and at 12:05 a.m. was called off until 7 a.m. As darkness settled over the area, the Tampa police helicopter, equipped with a powerful search light, was called into the area. Conducting the ground search for the youth were several sheriff's deputies, members of the Armsdale and Odessa volunteer fire departments, and over 100 residents. Searchers reported finding the boy's bicycle at 11 p.m. behind the 7-Eleven store, just off a path used by children to ride to the store.

"As the search progressed into the night, the store's parking lot became the hub of activity, packed with vehicles and volunteers. Wives of the searchers brought coffee, as night temperatures began dropping. Officials said there had been no positive indications that foul play was involved in the youth's disappearance. Officials could release no clothing description. The boy is described as being about four feet 11 inches in height and has auburn, wavy hair. The youth is the son of Gilbert and Lorraine Kushner. Kushner is chairman of the department of anthropology and associate dean of behavioral sciences at the University of South Florida. Residents of the area said the area in which the youth is believed lost is pocked with caves."

I felt sick as I read over the words. It was my life, my family, my brother, but at the same time, it didn't seem real. There was his name, my parents' names, my dad's job description, but how could this really be us? I felt dissociated, as if in a dream. I had been learning in my English literature class how details bring a story to life, and every single detail in this story was exploding with color before my eyes.

All my life, I had grown up with just that handful of memories, scattered frames of broken film. But now each sentence brought more frames of the film to light. When edited together with my own fleeting recollections, they formed lengthier strips of film, segments of memory that I saw in my mind's eye, as if they were now blurring before me on the microfilm machine screen:

My memory of talking with Jon on the sidewalk . . . 150 people begin a search around six at night . . . *My memory of standing outside my house giving a description of Jon's clothing to the police* . . . Women serving coffee to the volunteers . . . *My memory of playing whirlybird with Jon in our room* . . . A real police helicopter flying over our house with a searchlight . . . *Jon and me twirling the VertiBird plane around his room as we tried to rescue the orange plastic astronaut in his orange plastic raft* . . . Someone finding Jon's bike behind the 7-Eleven store . . . *Me at the controls, lowering the helicopter toward the astronaut's raft* . . . The light of the police helicopter switching off at midnight, and the volunteers going home . . . *Jon watching happily as the astronaut dangled from my VertiBird in the air.*

My time in the library sitting at the microfilm reader became a blur. One by one, I read the newspaper accounts and looked at the accompanying grainy photographs. "David sits in the kitchen with his parents, trying to understand what is happening." I read this line in one of the old newspaper stories from 1973. It was written by a reporter who had come to our house the day after Jon had disappeared, and it felt so weird. There I was in the moment, this four-year-old kid struggling to make sense of the chaos, and here I was now, some nine years later, still doing the same thing.

Each story gave me details I didn't have before: the way our house looked, comments my parents made to reporters, how the police and community organized the search, and so on. I drank them in thirstily, as my brain organized the details into scenes, images, dialogue, moments. I wanted to know what I didn't know, understand what I didn't understand, feel what I hadn't felt. Perhaps more than anything, I wanted to feel connected to this central experience, to my family, to Jon.

How long I was there, how many stories I read, I wouldn't recall. Maybe I was just there for one afternoon. Maybe I trudged back there several times over the course of a week. I didn't tell anyone what I was doing, didn't discuss it with my friends, my parents, or Andy. It was my own private wormhole. The screen became a portal to the past, just like one of my favorite sci-fi TV shows, *The Time Tunnel*. That short-lived series was about two guys who got stuck in their time machine, a spinning black-and-white spiral from which they couldn't escape. Each week, they'd end up in a different place—maybe the Old West or the French Revolution—and struggle for a way back. But now I was at the controls, twisting the knobs as I disappeared inside and watched the diorama materialize around me.

"It was a good scene when he left," my dad told a reporter. It was October 29, 1973, a day after Jon had gone missing. Dad was sitting in the kitchen, long hair and beard, smoking a cigarette, and staring at the floor. Friends and family milled around the room quietly. "He had just finished mowing the lawn," my dad went on. "He earned his buck and went to get some candy." Jon was a good kid, my dad said, not the kind to get into a car with a stranger. Before my brother left, he told me he'd call if it rained so that our dad could pick him up at the store. "The rains came at 3 p.m.," the reporter wrote. "The call never did."

At some point, my dad went out in the woods to search, but

called the Sheriff's Department around five after having found nothing. Volunteers and police combed the woods for hours. Andy was out there searching too. It wasn't until eleven o'clock that someone saw Jon's bike "half-hidden," as the reporter wrote, behind some bushes a ways off from the main path. Though the discovery of the bike led the police to suspect foul play, they initially dealt with it as a missing-person's case. The 7-Eleven clerk said that she might have seen Jon at her store, but couldn't recall. It seemed clear, however, that Jon—given his history, and that he had left his wallet at home—hadn't disappeared on his own. "From all outward appearances," said one official, "he is not a runaway."

By the next morning, the case was making headlines, and volunteers came from across the city to help search. A photographer shot a group of men and women gathered outside the 7-Eleven, dressed in jeans and sunglasses, some holding walking sticks, as a police officer pointed where to go. Officers rode horses through the woods, as members of a water rescue team waded through swamps and lakes. The wilderness that had long been a source of freedom and adventure became foreboding. "We used to run around a lot back there," one searcher told a reporter, "Kids used to dig up underground forts. One could cave in on you, and no one would ever know."

By later that day, however, Sheriff's Major Walter Heinrich told the crowd that "quite frankly, I think we have exhausted every technique in searching the terrain in this area."

By the next day, Halloween, the search expanded farther around north Tampa, with hundreds of volunteers going door-to-door distributing pictures of my brother and seeking clues. Many of the volunteers were from the University of South Florida, where my dad taught. Mitch Silverman, a colleague of my father's who chaired the Criminal Justice Department at USF and was a close family friend from the synagogue, told a reporter, "Large numbers of students, many of whom did not know Kushner, volunteered to join the search."

Mitch was a hulking, sweet man with an easy laugh whom I'd often see around our house. His wife, Cindy, was the therapist who had worked with Jon on his auditory processing difficulties. As I read his name in the paper and read the stories of the volunteers, another side of the story appeared to me, one I had not been seeking but found nonetheless: the volunteers, the people from across town who came to help and support my family.

In one article, my dad told a reporter about the two passersby who were just taking a walk when they saw the search party and joined in. I looked at the faces of the people in the woods, women pushing aside palm fronds, somehow finding the strength to do something so unthinkable for the sake of someone else. For years, I had built up a wall between myself and others when it came to Jon, a defensive fort against rumormongers and bullies. But by doing so, I had kept out, or at least not been aware of, the strangers and friends and neighbors around me who had done so much for us.

Another one of those mentioned in the articles was Arnie Levine, a close family friend and attorney who became, I discovered, instrumental that week. Up to this point, I had known that there was a special relationship between Arnie and my family, one that I didn't fully grasp other than that he was a lawyer who had helped us out. I had known Arnie's kids from IDS, and we spent many long, playful, and memorable Sundays at their house on the bay, swimming in their black-bottomed pool and having pillow fights. The Levines had a boat named *Olive*, and on other days, we'd sail off into the bay, climbing the mast and listening to Jimmy Buffett while everyone ate freshly boiled shrimp and laughed.

But here was another Arnie before me now, the man telling the reporter about the search party's door-to-door campaign. I pictured the long-haired college students walking up to houses around town, houses decorated with pumpkins and witches for Halloween. In a dark twist, the search was called off that night to, as the paper put it, "avoid confusion with Halloween festivities." Mitch, for one, was wearing down. "I never worked so hard and felt so useless," he told a reporter.

By the next day, November 1, the door-to-door search, which had covered thirty square miles but failed to turn up evidence, was called off. However, Mitch told reporters that they were not giving up. This was a grassroots effort, the kind of which the city hadn't been seen before. Over five thousand posters were being passed out to over forty businesses and government offices, and they were now being distributed as far as a hundred miles away, and soon made it as far as the borders of Georgia and Alabama. Volunteers raised $5,000 to offer as a reward for clues to Jon's whereabouts. The FBI was now on the case as well. The US Air Force dispatched planes with heat seeking equipment to scan the area.

On November 4, a week after Jon went missing, and still with no apparent leads, a *Tribune* reporter came to our house to interview my parents. The story ran with the headline "Missing Boy's Parents Keep Their Hope Alive." As I sat there in the school library looking at the page, numbness washed over me. There before me were pictures of my parents, pictures I'd never seen taken in the moment, grainy shots of black and white, showing them in our house, waiting. The photos made everything seem so real.

There was my mother: nine years younger, her dark hair a bit longer, her face slack, her eyes a bit puffy from what must have been a lack of sleep, or just the strain. "Every Day Is a New Day," read a quote from her underneath. Below it to the left was a close-up of my dad: tired eyes behind his glasses, curly, dark hair twisting above the frames, puffing a cigarette as a long ash hung. "Kushner Shows Tension of Waiting for Word from Son," this caption read. To the right was another shot of him, sitting on our striped recliner, the one that was still in our house all these years later, his hands crossed as he looked down at some papers, including a child's drawing of a smiley face, on the floor—papers identified in the caption as the letters of support from students at the Boys Academy.

The question the reporter and readers had then was almost certainly the same question I had now as I read the story: How could my parents survive this horror, this interminable wait, this nightmare? I had my own suppositions at thirteen, just from having grown up around them. In the years after Jon's death, I knew that they remained sensitive and open to life, that they cultivated a large support network of friends, family, and colleagues. I knew how much they loved to laugh and eat and celebrate the good times, how passionate they were about their work and the community around them. But even so, I had no idea how much of this was in place at the time Jon disappeared or, perhaps, how much of it had come as a result of that tragedy. I just knew that as much as I was searching for clues to my own story, one mystery seemed unfathomable: how they got through that week.

The reporter gave one account of my dad's answer during that interminable week. " 'We've been surviving on chemistry,' Kushner said, referring to the number of tranquilizers, stimulants, and coffee they've taken to hold up under the pressure. 'We get along, alone together,' Kushner said, 'and you cry and then you go back.' "

But that was just a part it. In the story, my dad went to great lengths to talk about the incredible support that came from the most disparate places. "The one colossal good is that there has been a tremendous coming together, that lumps together the cleavages that separate each other," he said. He spoke of the university crowd coming together with the police, the Jewish community with the non-Jews, the rich with the poor. My dad also spoke of the motorcycle biker who came to our house to help. The biker told my dad that he had his newly tuned cycle outside and wanted some "rough ground" to search. Later that day, the man returned, covered in mud, and told my dad, "Give me rougher ground."

My dad was not just a father who was missing a son. He was an anthropologist, filtering this experience through his trained eyes and mind. "I have come to realize fully," my dad went on to the reporter, "if we adults present [people with] alternative ways of being human and applying their humanity, then they'll use it."

The entire time I was reading the microfilm at the library, I knew what was coming. I didn't know all the details, but I knew how this story ended: with Jon's murder. But seeing the oversize headline on the front page of the *Tampa Tribune* from November 6, 1973, felt like a shock. "Body of Kushner Youth Found in Lonely Grave," it read.

I recoiled at the sight of the photos: the shot of the shrouded stretcher being carried into an ambulance, the photo of one of the two suspects being led somewhere in cuffs by the police. I absorbed enough of the story to confirm the few horrible details I knew, and perhaps, wanted to know: that Jon had suffocated on a gag and had been mutilated after he was dead. But I was too repulsed by the images of the killers to keep my eyes on the pages for very long.

Instead, I quickly twisted the black knob of the microfilm machine, blurring the subsequent days of headlines and pictures as they scrolled by. At one point, I passed a photo that caused me to stop and rewind. The headline of the story was "Jonathan Is Laid to Rest." It was a picture of my dad in his suit walking into our synagogue for the memorial service. I was walking beside him in my brown vest, slacks, and a checkered long-sleeve shirt that I recalled feeling like satin. I seemed to be looking up at my dad toward his downcast face, a face that I might have been scanning for clues. I was holding my father's hand.

21

THE NEWSPAPER stories confirmed at least some of my haziest recollections: that Jon had, in fact, gone to the store for candy, and that he had promised to call home if it rained. I returned to that last memory I had of my brother: the two of us on the sidewalk. I remembered how I made him promise not only to call if it rained, but also to call so that I could remind him to get me the candy. Because he never phoned, I had always assumed that he never made it to the 7-Eleven at all, and that the killers had gotten him on his way in. Knowing that my memories were grounded in some truth, as awful as the truth was, helped me feel more connected to Jon.

But all the new details, the descriptions and scenes that I read in the paper, stirred up another familiar emotion too: guilt. I couldn't help imagining what might have happened had I not pressed him so hard to get me the gum. Maybe he wouldn't have gone. Or maybe if I had protested more loudly, complaining that he wasn't going to let me go, he would have given in and stayed home. This game of what-if was easy and addictive to play, and I twisted every possibility around in my head like a Rubik's Cube. What if Jon had agreed to let me go with him? What if they wouldn't have attacked had they seen two of us? What if they'd gotten us both? What if, somehow, I could have saved him?

I felt guilty about feeling guilty, ashamed to draw attention to my feelings even if they were just inside my head. We spoke a lot about guilt in my house, but not related to Jon. Guilt was something that we joked about as a trait of being Jewish, how parents and grandparents would lament "You don't call, you don't write!" and so on. We had a gag gift in our living room: a small can of aerosol labeled Mrs. Rubenstein's Guilt-Remover Spray. It smelled like roses.

Beyond stirring up my guilt and confirming some of my vague memories, the articles had an unexpected effect too: creating even more mystery for me. Now that I knew some details surrounding Jon's disappearance, the empty pages of my book seemed even more barren. What exactly did these guys do to Jon? Who were they? How'd they get caught? Where were they now? I did gather, either from the stories or from my parents, that the killers were in prison, and that the older one, Witt, had been sentenced to death. But rather than upset myself or my parents by asking more questions, I left that alone.

The mystery didn't grow just over Jon's death. My questions concerned his short but full life. Ordinarily after someone dies, you talk about him or her eventually, sharing stories, laughs, memories, feelings that keep the person alive in your heart and mind. But because of the horror of Jon's death, that ability was almost completely erased in my family. The pain was too great for idle memories. Instead, the silence prevailed. I felt doubly challenged, however, because I didn't have the well of memories to dip into myself. I envied Andy and my parents for the memories of Jon that they had in their heads. I wanted those for myself. I wanted to know him. To feel him. I wanted to know who he was when he was alive. But I resigned myself to, at least for the time being, not knowing more at all.

At thirteen, I was now older than Jon had been, a bizarre concept to me that seemed almost like something out of one of my comic books: how a little brother is transformed into a big brother. And because I was thirteen, I was becoming a bar mitzvah. As I stood on the bimah giving my bar mitzvah speech, looking out on the room full of friends and family, the memorial banners for Jon hanging in the lobby, I knew that many of them might be thinking the same thing as me when I thanked Jon for inspiring me with his memory: that I was becoming a man, while Jon would remain, forever, a boy.

22

THE DISTANCE between our sliding glass doors and the garbage cans outside around the corner of the house was maybe fifteen feet. But those fifteen feet I had to walk every night when taking out the kitchen trash felt like an eternity.

Despite my burgeoning sense of freedom and adventure, I felt plagued by the dark side of possibility: the fact that while anything could happen in the best possible sense, terrible things could happen too—like getting attacked and killed by a stranger while I was taking out the trash. The usual reassurances—say, the rarity of someone getting hit by lightning, the unlikelihood of dying in a car crash—were easy for me to dismiss. As wildly unusual as it was for Jon to die the way he did, the fact was that it had happened. And if something like that could happen to him, why couldn't something equally terrible, no matter how unlikely, happen to me?

My fear of getting murdered while taking out the trash was the most frequent reminder of this trauma. The paranoia became so intense that I began asking my dad or mom to wait for me by the sliding doors while I completed my chore outside. This went on long past the point of embarrassment, long after I began feeling that I was too old for such behavior. I never recalled them trying to talk me out of this or convince me that everything was going to be okay. Instead, what I felt from them was perhaps quiet compassion, an understanding that, as well as we were all getting along in our lives, we were still wounded, still raw, still feeling our way through the dark.

I began to think of this fear as the bogeyman. The bogeyman was bad. He had gotten my brother, and he was coming for me. He was this shadowy presence in the world, an evil, a chaos, something lurking in the woods, a phantom spirit able to move easily between the physical and spiritual realms. Maybe he was hiding behind the trash can, or maybe he had miniaturized and traveled into my brain, a little Darth Vader flying into my head like the crew from the sixties sci-fi flick *Fantastic Voyage*. But the bogeyman was always there waiting, and he had a way of coming at the most inopportune times.

I developed strange fears, fears even of myself. As a kid, I had the incredibly nerdy hobby of collecting magnets and ball bearings. I kept my three largest ball bearings in a medicine bottle in a drawer. But slowly I became fixated on them. I began getting consumed by an uncontrollable urge to swallow the ball bearings and choke myself. I had never felt suicidal before, and didn't understand if this was some such impulse now. The weird fear became so bad that I considered throwing out the ball bearings but couldn't bear to part with them. Instead, I handed them to my mom one day and asked her to keep them in her room. I'm sure she had no idea what I was talking about or why I was behaving so urgently, but I couldn't help myself. I needed the fear away from me.

I was also afraid for my parents. Once, I was at school when

I saw an ambulance race down the street. As the sirens faded, I felt an icy wave of fear pass through my body: a conviction that the ambulance was carrying one of my parents; that something horrible had happened, and they were dead or dying. The fear became so intense that it ceased to be fear at all. It was reality. My reality. My parents. They had died. They were dying. I knew it. And there was nothing I could do but sit there in class and pretend like I was paying attention to whatever the teacher was saying. But nothing could distract my belief that something terrible was happening.

In these moments, the pot didn't help. One night when I was fifteen, something darker rose from the smoke. It happened when my parents were out for the evening, and I was home alone. The minute they walked out the door, I headed urgently for my room. By now I had Rush posters completely covering my walls, along with a giant light blue satin Rush banner—of the man-in-the-red-star logo—that I had bought at the Wooden Nickel head shop. My prized possession—my stereo components (tape deck, turntable, speakers)—shimmered on my chest of drawers, underneath my shelf of Mad magazines and Tolkien books.

I opened my closet and fished out the tennis ball can in which I stashed my pot. As I opened the lid, the gust of sweet herbal stickiness hit my nose. I had plenty of options for how to get high. The water pipe was my favorite, able to cool the smoke and not require heavy cleanup. I also had a little gold serpentine pipe, one that, I discovered, could be used to smoke pot underwater, almost like a periscope, in our redwood hot tub out back. In my closet, I'd also stashed away a bong, a once-translucent cylinder with twisty green plastic tubes and a sticky film of resin on the bottom. I also had plenty of joints: tightly wound numbers that I had learned to roll from watching a Cheech and Chong movie.

Grabbing a joint, I went out back and sucked down a few hits as my cat watched me without judgment. Then I sucked down a few more hits for good measure. I could smoke a lot—maybe because I had built up a tolerance. Smoking thirteen bong hits was my record. By the time I walked back into my room to put away my paraphernalia, the air was thicker, slower, groovier around me, and the familiar fuzzy goodness was enveloping me again.

High and relaxed, I settled in alone for a night of TV, enduring *The Love Boat* to get to *Fantasy Island* and hoping to stay up late enough for *Saturday Night Live.* But as I lay on the couch munching on mini egg rolls, the doorbell rang. This rarely happened at night, and it sent a shiver through my body, pumping up my heart with blood and sending it off to the races. *Who the fuck would be ringing at eleven o'clock on Saturday night?* I thought. It rang again. Then came a knock.

Killing the lights, I went into stealth mode, tiptoeing across the shag carpet for the door in paranoia. I could hear muffled voices of men outside, and more loud knocks. Fuck the peephole, I thought, this was bad. I slithered past the nearby windows, beelining through the kitchen into a bedroom down the hall. *Who are these men? What do they want? Why aren't they leaving?* The questions raced through my mind uncontrollably, looping around and around as the fear spread, filling me, pooling from the edge of my toes up to the top of my skull.

Then I heard them talking. I pressed my ear close to the window, and could make out a few scattered words here and there: "What are we going to do?" one said. "He's going to see it when he gets back." *See it? See what?* I wondered. And then the bogeyman in my head conjured the answer, letting the film play before me. I saw a dark patch in the woods outside our house, and my parents were dead there. These men had killed them, buried them in a shallow grave, and now they were coming for me. They wanted no witnesses, no evidence. And they were worried about me or someone else seeing what they had done. I was sure of it.

It seemed like the knocking went on forever, unrelenting, increasingly urgent. And I couldn't take it anymore. I marched into the back of the house, grabbed the phone, and called my friend Dave. "Dude!" I whispered breathlessly into the mouthpiece, "I need you to come over!"

"Why?" Dave asked.

"I don't know, man," I said. "There are these guys outside my house, and they won't leave. They keep knocking and ringing the doorbell."

"What do they want?"

"I don't know!" I said louder, and then quieted myself back down. "That's the whole thing, I don't know what's going on, and I'm freaking out." I paused. "And I'm really stoned." Too stoned, I suppose in hindsight, to worry too much about my friend's safety, and how maybe I had just called him over to confront a bunch of murderous thugs. Or so stoned, I guess, that my friend realized I was just deep into a psychosomatic bender.

"I'll be right over," Dave said.

Minutes later, I heard the doorbell ring again. Then I could hear Dave's voice outside, talking to the men. "No, someone is home," he told them. Taking a deep breath, I straightened my hair and opened the door casually as if—despite the fact that they had been knocking for over a half hour—I had just heard the knock for the first time. Outside, I saw Dave with two clean-cut middle-aged guys. "We didn't think anyone was home," one of them said pleasantly.

"Oh no," I lied, forcing a smile. "I had my headphones on." My eyes darted around the yard behind them, looking for signs of their crime. But there was nothing.

"Is that your car parked out front?" one of them asked.

I looked in the distance and saw my dad's orange Ford Mustang. "Yeah," I said. "Why?"

"We were driving by and didn't see it, and clipped the side of it," one of the guys said apologetically. "It's dented pretty bad."

A wave of relief passed over me. My parents were alive! These guys weren't murderers! They were just friendly neighbors coming clean about their accident. I was so elated by the news that my parents hadn't been murdered that I must have seemed insanely happy to hear that our car had just been smashed. "Oh!" I said gingerly. "That's fine! No problem!" I might have even said that it was great.

After they gave me their insurance details and left, I invited Dave inside. I told him everything, how I had gotten high and my imagination had run away with me. Then my voice kind of trailed off. Despite the fact that my family's story was so well known in Tampa, I rarely, if ever, discussed it with my friends. It was just too personal, too intense, and I just didn't want to call attention to our history—perhaps thinking that if I didn't, I could be as "normal" as anyone else. But by the way Dave reacted, by his patience, his understanding, by the fact that he didn't make fun of me, as boys often do with each other—all that told me that he probably knew what was going on after all. This gave me an incredible sense of comfort. Even in my craziest moments, I realized, I didn't have to be alone.

But I never considered myself religious. How could there be a God who would let a child be murdered? Reluctantly, I accompanied my parents to the synagogue's annual cemetery service. We stood outside with a few dozen other congregants under a tent that barely kept out the heat and humidity. It brought back a lot of old feelings standing there, feeling like an open wound, some hideous gash of a person being picked at by everyone around me. They all knew our story. Generations knew our story. And I hated the attention—everyone loses someone—we just lost someone in a particularly brutal and sensational way. Death is death.

I half listened to the rabbi's sermon until something he said caught my attention. He kept mentioning the word *remembrance*. This was a memorial service, a service about remembering. "We consecrate this hour the memory of our departed" . . . "We recall" . . . "We remember" . . . "May their memories endure among us as a lasting benediction" . . . "In tribute to their memory, I pledge to perform acts of charity and goodness." The name of this service in Hebrew was Yizkor—it meant "remember." Remembering was divine. We were there to participate in that divine act.

But I felt like an amnesiac. The few memories I had of Jon, particularly my most vivid and meaningful one on the sidewalk, were suspect. All I really had were memories of his death: the newspaper articles, the fear, the silence, the crying, the tranquilizers, the screams, the needing my parents to wait for me at the sliding glass door while I took out the garbage at night, the little brown box of his possessions high up on the shelf in his old room, the conviction that I or someone close to me would die a gruesome and horrible death, that we wouldn't live long, that something always had to go wrong, that though one killer was sentenced to die and the other to life behind bars, their rampage would continue. So much was missing.

The service ended. My parents and I made our way over to Jon's headstone. It was a small grave beneath a tree—one of the few shaded spots in the cemetery. The Jewish custom is to put a small rock on a headstone to show that you've been there. I fumbled around for just the right rock, as if there were just the right one. We came to the site and set the rocks on the headstone. My mom and dad cried. But I never cried at this spot. I never felt anything. Jon was cremated after he died—a decision made with the help of the rabbi, because my parents couldn't fathom the pain of burying him—and his ashes were spread over Tampa Bay by a family friend in a helicopter. My family erected this headstone in Jon's honor. But when I looked down at the grave, I saw nothing. I could get down on my knees, claw through the dirt, the rocks, the roots, but he wouldn't be there. No matter how hard I tried, I would not find a trace of my brother.

23

ONE DAY in March 1985, I got caught at high school forging guidance office passes. I was a senior, and had used a fake pass to pull a girl out of class and ask her to the prom. I thought it was a clever way to ask her out, but it backfired. Not only did she turn me down because she already had a date, but she also told her teacher what I had done, and I got busted. The school suspended me for a day—the same day, it turned out, that Johnny Paul Witt, the older of the two men who'd killed my brother, was scheduled to be executed.

Witt's execution had become politically charged, a national story and a precedent-setting case in the burgeoning debate over capital punishment. Two years earlier, his sentence had been overturned by the US Court of Appeals for the Eleventh Circuit after it was revealed that a prospective juror was dismissed for failing to reveal her opposition to the death penalty. Later, following a debate at the US Supreme Court, the court reinstated the sentence with a historic vote that made it easier to remove such jurors from capital punishment cases. The night before Witt's trip to the electric chair, nicknamed "Big Sparky," Thurgood Marshall and two other justices lost their bid to postpone it. Witt would become just the twelfth person executed in Florida since the state reinstituted the death penalty in the 1970s.

On the morning of March 6, I woke early and walked out to the patio to sit with my dad, who was listening to the news on a transistor radio. I'm not sure where my mom was. Andy was off at college. I opened the sliding glass door and saw my dad sitting on a white plastic chair, smoking a cigarette and staring off into the trees. "Maybe you were meant to be home today," he said as I pulled up a chair.

Up until that point, my dad and I still didn't talk much about Jon. Perhaps I was being overprotective of him, hesitant to bring up the topic. But my brother's death still seemed too painful for him—even given his involvement with the grief support groups. And none of us ever talked about Jon's killers. The killers existed in some dark fog—out there, but not out there, monsters too nightmarish to conjure. It got to the point where I didn't even know what my parents knew at all. Did they know what had really happened to Jon? Did they know why he was chosen? As we sat on the patio waiting for the hour of the execution to come, my father said it was time I learned the full story.

"I don't know how much you know about what happened to Jon," he began. I told him I remembered that Jon had been hit in the head, gagged, and then suffocated in the trunk of the car. I had also heard something about mutilation, but that was it. Because Jon had never called me as he'd promised, I assumed he had been abducted on his way *to* the 7-Eleven that morning. This would also explain why no one reported finding the candy that I had asked him to get me.

But it didn't take long for my story to unravel, as my dad told me his account of what happened. Jon *had* made it to the store, he said. On the way back, Witt and Tillman hit him with the pipe. They gagged him and threw him in the back of their car's trunk. They drove to a secluded spot in the woods in another part of town and removed Jon from the car. They were startled to find that he had suffocated and died. They had planned to torture him alive.

Off in the woods, the two of them raped his dead body. They cut off his genitals, which they buried in a small bag as a souvenir. Then they left him in a shallow grave in an orange grove. Sometime later, my dad said, Witt's wife turned him in. That day, the sheriff on the case, Sheriff's Major Heinrich, climbed up a ladder and onto the roof of a burger place where Witt was working. Heinrich, who became very close with my family, later told my dad that he put his hand on his gun as he approached Witt. If the suspect so much as raised his wrench, the sheriff said, he would have shot him dead.

But Witt, to what I took to be Heinrich's and my dad's disappointment, didn't resist. He was arrested and found guilty of murder. Tillman, his accomplice, received a life sentence because he was diagnosed as schizophrenic, and the lawyers feared that if they tried for a death sentence, he'd get off on an insanity plea. But Witt's final day, today, had come at last, twelve years after the crime.

Learning all this felt terrifying. For years, I'd heard awful rumors about Jon's death and never knew what to believe. Now, at sixteen, I realized some of the most terrible stories were true. When I told my dad, for the first time, about my last memory of Jon, sadness and compassion filled his eyes. The memory wasn't real, he said gently. When Jon left, I had been inside the house playing. The last person to see him alive was my dad.

What? My mind reeled. I had spent my childhood building a narrative around that final exchange with my brother, imbuing it with meaning. I had been so much wrapped up in that memory because it connected me to Jon. It also filled me with guilt. For years, I had harbored the shitty feeling that maybe if I hadn't asked him for the candy, he wouldn't have gone to the 7-Eleven that day. I even remembered giving my deposition to the cops, telling them what Jon wore, what he said, where he was going. How could all that be wrong?

Maybe my dad had the story wrong, I told him. But he was sure he was right. In fact, he went on, when they found the candy that Jon had bought that day, there wasn't any Snappy Gator Gum. There were just a few things Jon had bought for himself, and also something he had bought my mom and dad. How could this be? I wondered.

Maybe Jon knew what I wanted but didn't get it. Suddenly I felt something primal: sibling rivalry. How could he not get me what I wanted? The anger, rather than leaving me feeling guilty, felt strangely comforting. It was just an honest brotherly emotion, and all my life I just wanted to feel any kind of emotion involving Jon, even this.

But as the anger and guilt passed, I was left sitting outside with something else coursing through my brain: confusion. Why would I go to such lengths to make up this story to myself about Jon? Maybe I had written my own piece of fiction as some weird kind of consolation. I felt lost, but also sickened by the details my dad told me about Jon's murder. I thought about all those years of kids telling me that Jon had been cut up and put in a pickle jar, and realized that they were sort of right. What else were they right about? I wondered. What else did they know that perhaps my family didn't know?

The new details raised only more questions: Who were these killers? Why had they done what they did? Why did I tell myself this elaborate lie? How could I find the answers? A new world of mystery opened before me, and I had no idea how to solve it. I felt disconnected from my community, my father, my family, myself—even from Jon.

At 7:10 a.m., the moment of Witt's electrocution, my dad checked the time. "He's dead now," he said.

Part 3

24

BEFORE LONG, I was off to the University of Maryland, and the distance opened up a new dialogue with my father. Though we were always close, the space between us that represented Jon didn't fill until I was gone, and my dad could put his feelings in words in letters to me.

Sometimes it was a national tragedy that inspired him to write about Jon. In August 1990 a serial killer murdered five students at the University of Florida. "I think of the parents," my father wrote me, referring to the mother and father of one of the murdered girls. "The parents weren't allowed to view the body because it was mutilated," he went on, "and of course we're all brought right back into our own experience. It isn't very far beneath the surface, is it? Doesn't take a whole lot to bring it up, still raw, so painful."

A few months later, on October 29, he wrote Andy and me on the seventeenth anniversary of Jon's death, which had come the day before. "It kind of sneaked up on me, as sometimes happens," he wrote. "Sometimes I await it for weeks, looking for the weather to change too. Very often, it seems, just days before the

28th, it begins to get a little cooler here, sometimes a lot cooler . . . Anyway, yesterday was 17 years, hard to believe, in one sense, and, as ever, not so hard to believe at all, seems so very long ago, and yet, I can still, if I focus on it, relive much of it . . . So, here we all are, having survived Jon's death willingly or unwillingly, and I hope we've each of us somehow learned from it something to help us continue living . . . And now back to the workday world. It's always strange realizing the world doesn't know or care, by and large."

Other times, he'd suggest books on grief for me to read, such as Viktor Frankl's *Man's Search for Meaning*, which he described as being "aimed at transforming (not transcending . . .) suffering, i.e., suffering (loss, grief, etc.) disorganizes one's life. Everything's a shambles, no structure, no meaning. So, one has to find meaning, says Victor. Other folks say one has to find structure. Others say the love of a person or several. Others say God. The common matter is suffering, as you said, and searching for meaning is one way to transform it into something positive."

One fall day five years later, Andy and I received a letter from Dad that took me aback. "Enclosed is a letter received right before the holiday weekend," he wrote. "At the moment I tend to think Mom and I will not write a letter, we certainly won't attend the hearing, although I'll find out when it will occur. But I don't really know at this point, we might decide to write something. In any case, you each are free to do what you wish about this. Love, Dad."

Stapled to his note was a letter from the Florida Parole Commission regarding Gary Tillman. It had been twelve years since Witt was executed, and Tillman was serving his life sentence. "I regret having to bring up the past and memories that I am sure you would just as soon not have to deal with all over again," the victims' services administrator wrote. "However, as a victim, you have a right to be heard in the parole process. The inmate will be interviewed by the Commission in May 1997 and then the Commission will hold a public hearing to set a tentative parole date for him." We were invited to attend the hearing and, if we so desired, write a letter or speak. "Once the Commission sets a parole date for the inmate, they must review the case at least every two years to determine if any change of his date is warranted." The victims' services administrator concluded by apologizing "if this letter upsets you—and I can certainly understand how it would—but I do want you to know of your rights as a victim."

I had no idea that Tillman—whose name I could still barely say or think—was even eligible for parole. With Witt having been executed ten years before, we took solace in knowing that Tillman, at least, would never get out. But once again the memories I thought to be true were proven to be wrong, just like the memory of talking with Jon on the sidewalk the day of his murder. There's a terrible, emptying feeling that sucks the air from you when you learn that something you held true and meaningful isn't true at all. For me, the vacuum filled with old fears and paranoia. What if Tillman actually got out? Would he come after my family again, or me?

It also felt like history repeating itself because, just as my parents were having a peak year when Jon was killed, it had been, up until this moment, a peak year for me. Now twenty-seven, I was finally feeling like I was living my dreams. I had recently married and moved to a one-bedroom apartment on a leafy street in the Cobble Hill section of Brooklyn. I was writing for *Rolling Stone* and other magazines, a goal I'd had since reading Hunter S. Thompson in college, and was covering the nascent digital culture after having worked for an early internet start-up. But none of that mattered now. I was back on the sidewalk with my brother again, looking into the woods.

When I called my parents, they said that they were as surprised by the news as me. We spoke quietly, and with long pauses. Perhaps it was part of the post-traumatic stress, but, to some degree, I was still dissociating from Jon's murder, living my life, pursuing adventures, riding a bike in my imagination far away from the woods by my childhood home in Tampa where he died. But moments like this brought it all back, the weight of the murder and how it subdued my parents' voices, the sort of humbleness we felt to the chaos of life, the evil that existed, the brother and son who was swallowed alive.

My parents told me they had already spoken with Andy, who said he wanted to attend the hearing and make a statement on behalf of the family against Tillman's release. But, again, they weren't going to go themselves. I didn't need to ask why. I knew that this was too painful for them, that they didn't want to relive it at the hearing, and that, of course, they were putting no pressure on us.

My next call was to Andy, who was now working as a musician and had a family of his own. Though my brother and I had grown up eight years apart, we'd become closer in recent years. We had caught up on lost time, discovering a shared taste in music, movies, and food. There was something ineffable between us, a bond that went deep through the loss of Jon and connected us. I know that he'd had his own unique struggles to deal with the horror of Jon's murder in a way that didn't cripple him or prevent his own child from getting the most out of life.

When I reached him by phone, Andy was as floored as the rest of us; completely caught off guard by the letter and hearing. He had already made a few calls to Florida Commission on Offender Review's Victims Services department, and learned that the parole hearing was a result of a legal loophole. Though Florida law now denied the possibility of parole to such murderers, Tillman had been sentenced before that law was put into effect and was therefore eligible for release. Since his incarceration, Tillman had a clean prison record, Andy told me, except for one sexual offense. There was no way of knowing how the court would rule. So Andy had decided to fly down for the hearing in a few months and say whatever he could to keep Tillman in jail. I didn't have to go if I didn't want to, he added, it was up to me.

But I already knew my answer: I wanted to go speak too. After a lifetime of feeling impotent about my brother's murder, I was suddenly in a position to take action. Andy and I were just kids when Jon died, after all. There was only so much we could do then. Andy had done what he could at thirteen: he joined the search party, combed the woods, took me trick-or-treating while Jon was missing to give me a sense of normalcy. All I could do at the time was try to make sense of the senseless. But now here we were: grown men, grown brothers, best friends. And we could do something if we wanted. We could speak. It felt like we were walking into the schoolyard to defend our brother against the neighborhood bully. It was time to fight.

Soon after our decision, our dad wrote us a letter. "How very tough all this is on all of us," he wrote. "We're so struck with your willingness to appear at that dreadful situation and can understand why you each want to be there. My appearance on TV, my answering our phone that was being monitored by the FBI and talking to all sorts of maniacs who called, etc etc was all my effort, I guess, to try to do something, so I certainly understand your concerns and am grateful for them, so is Mom, we feel like we're in the middle of a castle with very strong walls and you guys are out there on your horses in armor defending us."

And just like that, we were back in this as a family again. The years of silence had pushed away and left us here in a new kind of battle again. On the suggestion of Andy's therapist—who was surprised by how little we had discussed Jon's death as a family—we had a family therapy session. It would be the first time we'd discussed Jon so directly together in our lives. We made our way to the psychologist's office. My parents and Andy sat on a soft leather couch, and I sat in a chair beside them. To be there together in this moment had a power that I can still feel as I'm writing this sentence now. It was a deep sense of presence, of stillness, the sadness and weight of the loss there between us.

The session went on for two hours, and now resides in a place like a dream. There was crying, and stillness, as we went through the experience, but I have no idea what we said. All I remember is that at some point, Andy asked some question of my father, and my father said that he couldn't go to the place that Andy was asking him to go. It was too painful. He'd spent decades trying to get out of that place, and he wasn't going to go back. The session left me with a greater realization and understanding of how truly separate each of us was in our grief, in our relationships with Jon and Jon's murder. But as separate as we were, we were always a family, and, now, bound together in this with love.

While our parents entrusted us to the hearing, Andy and I agreed that there was one place we would go together as brothers without them. We wanted to know the full facts of Jon's death. Though Andy and I never spoke much about the details of Jon's murder, it was clear that he knew little more than I did. Just as I had been letting my imagination torment me all these years with what might have happened to Jon, Andy had been enduring that stress too.

In a way, both of us had resigned ourselves to the experience of not knowing the truth, to compartmentalizing the horror of the murder as self-preservation. But that self-preservation—the self-delusion, in a sense—had come at a price. Because we didn't know what happened, the mystery festered in our minds and souls. Maybe now, by learning the details, as horrific as they might be, we would find not only some peace but also, most importantly, the empowerment to speak out against one of the men who had done this.

When the hearing was a few months away, we called a victim's rights advocate and asked her if it was possible to hear the police report about Jon's murder. She told us she could arrange it. We also began hitting the phone, tracking down former cops and lawyers who had been involved with the case. I pored over newspaper articles I'd long forgotten or missed. Andy and I both thought we knew the basic details —that Jon had been hit with a lead pipe, put in a trunk, suffocated to death, and then mutilated. But we didn't know the details beyond that, and we wanted to be done with them now. I was tired of imagining what had happened to Jon. I wanted to know the truth.

Soon I was traveling on an Amtrak train to Andy's house so that we could be together when we heard the details from the case report. I sat there for what seemed like days, listening to the new Radiohead CD, *OK Computer,* over and over again like some kind of meditation. "Rain down, rain down," Thom Yorke sang, as I watched the forest blur past the window. "Come on rain down on me. From a great height."

The next day, Andy and I descended into his basement office, a carpeted room with Andy's musical equipment—guitars, a piano—and a shelf lined with books. He had a picture of Jon there, the school photo that had become so iconic, of him smiling, in the red shirt, his head tilted slightly, the red hair. Andy picked up his speakerphone and set it on a small table between where we sat.

"Are you ready?" he asked me as he dialed the number.

"Yeah," I said, my heart beginning to race. Then the empathetic voice of the victim's services worker, a woman, came on the phone. She began reading from a statement Tillman had made decades before when he had led the cops to the crime scene.

For three decades, Jon's story was the central puzzle of my life. I had a few pieces here, a few there, but the rest was missing. Now, after weeks of preparing, reading, talking, I pieced together the puzzle of Jon's death inside my mind like never before. As I sat there in Andy's basement, the walls began to fade to black, trees grew up from the ground around me, and I was there, watching my brother's murder unfold.

25

WAKE ME UP if anybody comes through," Witt told Tillman, according to court documents.

It was around twelve thirty in the afternoon on Sunday, October 28, 1973, and Tillman and Witt were parked in Witt's yellow Plymouth Satellite Sebring in the woods behind the 7-Eleven. They'd been there for a short time, snacking on Twinkies, Cracker Jacks, and Cokes while they waited for a victim. Witt said that he preferred a girl, thirteen to fifteen, but he'd take "whatever came along." If they got a girl, he wanted to slit her open from her crotch up with a knife. If they got a boy, he wanted to shoot him full of bows and arrows. Witt wanted to rape the child too.

Witt had climbed into the backseat to nap and told Tillman to wake him if he saw someone they could get. Witt grew irritated with the volume of Tillman's chewing. "Be quiet and let me sleep," Witt told him, "and stop making noises like a pig with your food."

Tillman soon began to doze off too, until he saw Jon pedal up to the store on his red bike and go inside. When he roused Witt and asked him if he wanted to attack this kid, Witt replied, "Might as well; I can't sleep." Grabbing his bow and arrows, Witt climbed from the car and handed Tillman a foot-long metal bit from a drill. "When the boy comes back," Witt told Tillman, "you know what to do." Tillman was to hit the kid, and if he missed, or if someone else came along, Witt would shoot the victim with the bow and arrow.

He pointed Tillman to a spot in the weeds nearby, where he was to crouch and wait. "You know what these kind of weeds do to me," Tillman said.

"You're sneezing because you won't get medicine for hay fever," Witt replied, and he chastised Tillman's condition for often screwing up their hunting missions. "You know, we might be able to find some game once in a while if you would get off your ass and get some medicine."

Jon soon left the store and began pedaling back "like he was trying to race somebody," Tillman recalled later to the police. As the boy approached, Tillman leapt from the bushes, and hit him on the back of the head with the drill bit. Jon coasted on for another ten feet or so before falling off his bike. Tillman quickly ran over to my brother, placing his hand over his mouth as Witt came over and began choking him. Afraid that Jon would draw attention to them, they bound him with plastic line and, on Witt's suggestion, gagged him with a T-shirt from a motorcycle shop. Witt propped up Jon's bike against a tree and rubbed off his fingerprints. Then they put Jon in the trunk of the car on an old yellow and blue rubber raft, and drove off.

They went up Busch Boulevard and then stopped at another 7-Eleven, where Witt bought a pack of cigarettes. Then they drove on a few miles, turning down a desolate road until they pulled up to a trash dump in an orange grove. When they opened the trunk, Tillman recalled later, Witt felt for a pulse. "Bet he's dead," he said. Then: "He is dead." Witt, who'd wanted to shoot him with arrows and torture him alive, was disappointed that that gag seemed to have suffocated him. "Dumbass," Witt told Tillman. "You tied it too tight."

As Tillman lifted the body from the trunk, Witt grabbed his bow and arrows. After checking the area to make sure they were alone, Witt searched Jon's pockets and was disappointed to find only three cents. He pulled off Jon's pants and cut his underwear loose with a six-inch hunting knife. Then he used the knife to start digging a hole, dumping the dirt in a bucket that they carried and emptied nearby. He handed Tillman the knife and told him to keep digging. While Tillman dug, he saw Witt trying to have sex with the dead body. The anus was too small, so Witt asked Tillman for the knife, and cut it open to make it larger. Tillman told police later that he didn't think Witt was able to complete the sex act. He also said that he tried to have sex with the corpse as well.

The two sat there for about fifteen minutes. Then they decided just to bury him in the shallow grave. At one point, they heard what sounded like a truck door close, and Witt scurried up a tree to look while Tillman kept digging. After laying the body in the hole, Witt took the knife and cut off Jon's penis and scrotum, putting them in a plastic bag. Tillman cut off the green and white Camp Keystone patch, which had a little blue owl on it, and kept it. "It was just a natural thing to do," he told the cops later. Concerned that the body would bloat above the earth and be exposed, they made small cuts in Jon's stomach. Tillman pushed too hard at one point, and the intestines spilled out onto the body. They threw dirt over the corpse, covering it as best they could, and went to leave.

Witt later transferred the penis and scrotum into a small brown Sinutab bottle, which he'd filled with alcohol to "pickle it," as he told Tillman. He had also told Tillman that if they had gotten a girl, he wanted to cut off her nipples and make a bracelet out of it. Five days later, on Friday, November 2, the two drove up to Withlacoochee State Forest, near a campsite they had frequented in the past. There by a fencepost, they buried the jar as a souvenir.

Three days later, on November 5, Witt's wife, Donna, turned in her husband after he'd made a drunken confession. And she had evidence. "Ms. Witt said that Witt and Tillman had brought home salt water taffy and Snappy Gator candy on 10/28/73," the police report read. "The deputies recalled that this was Jonathan's favorite candy, and he was going to the store to get some for his brother when he disappeared."

26

I WAS ON the same train riding home to New York City, watching the same trees, listening to the same Radiohead CD. I was in the same body, spinning on the same planet in the same universe. But I was different. I wasn't the same me. I could feel myself changing, unsettled by the details of Jon's murder and the evidence—the candy—that they had brought back to Witt's trailer.

I still didn't know if I'd had that conversation with Jon on the sidewalk as I had long recalled, or if it had been a figment of my imagination, as my dad suggested. But now I knew that he had at least bought the stuff at the store and that, horrifically, it had been found in Witt's home. This bizarre fate of the candy felt almost as sickening as the gory details; it was all so evil, so distressing, an even darker version of what had long felt like a Grimm's fantasy made real.

My mind blended the images disturbingly: the candy and my brother, Jon's neck being squeezed as his mouth gaped open with a T-shirt gagged inside, the candy neck being squeezed as the gator jaws opened with gumballs inside. As hard as I tried to fight off the images, to stop making this twisted connection in my imagination, they tormented me.

As I rode home on the train, the details were chemicals injected into my bloodstream, reshaping my mind, my memory, my consciousness. The movie wouldn't stop playing in my head. It adopted a soundtrack, the Radiohead song "Paranoid Android." Now when the slow part came, when Thom Yorke sang, "Rain down, rain down . . ." I kept seeing the same thing: the two men in the woods retrieving a plastic bag with pieces of my brother inside.

All my life, I had wanted the details. The details would kill my imagination, I'd hoped. Imaginations run wild without details. Imaginations imagine the most unimaginable things. Knives, bows, arrows, car trunks, bogeymen, bicycles, a little boy, a gag. Now after hearing excerpts of the police report, and later reading it myself, I had the facts. Things I thought I knew became corrected. He wasn't hit with a lead pipe, as I'd always thought, it was a foot-long drill bit. I took solace in knowing that Jon had not suffered long. He had died because the gag was too tight, and he had choked on his tongue. But now I knew where the killers had parked, how they waited, how they crouched, how they attacked, how Jon struggled, how they put him in the trunk, the disappointment they felt over his death, the knife, the mutilation, the necrophilia.

And the more I knew, the worse I felt. I didn't want to know anymore. I wanted to know again what it was not to know. I wanted to go back to the simple narrative I had long accepted: hit in the head, died in the trunk, abstract mutilation, the silvery blur of a knife in the air. I wanted to imagine a story that ended in darkness; the story I had grown up with all along. I wanted the version where I watched Jon pedal away, and his death came quickly in shadows. I wanted to be wrapped in the familiar blanket of darkness.

I wouldn't remember how I reacted sitting there in Andy's basement hearing the police report. I wouldn't remember if I cried, or what I asked, or what Andy and I discussed in the moments after the victim's services woman hung up. It was only the next day, sitting in the Amtrak train as the woods blurred by, that realizations set in like a flood. First, I thought about the kids at school, the ones who'd told me about a bow and arrow, and what I hoped were other rumors at the time. They had been right, more or less. Witt had brought a bow and arrow to the murder scene, but just hadn't ended up using it. They had known what I didn't know. I had warded them off with silence, with pretending not to hear, but I was warding off the truth. I was defenseless.

Then I thought about the strangulation. For years, my family had been told that Jon didn't suffer, that he had been knocked unconscious and suffocated in the trunk, that he didn't know what was happening to him. But this didn't seem to be the real story. Perhaps my family had been spared. Perhaps in a moment of incredible sympathy, in an impulse of humanity, the cops had gathered to discuss how much to tell my mom and dad, and they chose to leave out the hardest part of all: that the boy had been aware, if only for seconds, that he had struggled, that the large and murderous hands gripped his small neck.

Now that I had this information, what was I going to do with it? I felt horrified at having to share it with my parents. The roles now felt reversed. They had spent years protecting me from the details, sparing me from learning things that might haunt me. They loved me dearly, so dearly that they thought sparing me would make life easier somehow, less terrifying, less paralyzing. And now I was the parent, and they were the children. I was in the blinding sun, and they were in the shadows.

I wanted to keep them there. I wanted them to live the rest of their days just as they had done so far, taking sanctity in the comfort that their boy had not suffered. Because to have suffered was to have been aware, and to have been aware was to have known that—in that familiar thicket of woods so close to home, while his little brother waited, and his father watched football—he was being killed. I decided not to say anything; at least, not unless they asked. And if they asked, I supposed, I would figure out what to do then.

But in that decision, I felt a kind of loneliness I had never felt before. The loneliness of the protector. The loneliness of being an adult, stuck inside your own head, aware of things that you cannot control, aware of details altering your biochemistry, lacerating your insides, rearranging that which had already seemed to be arranged, reassembling you in a new form, like some Cubist painting, your eyes and ears shifted on your face, your foot where your head should be. It was the loneliness of returning to the world you had always known in a form you did not recognize or desire. And the only thing that felt lonelier was that to everyone else, you most likely looked the same.

I returned to Brooklyn as a transparency. I was clear through, like a paramecium, a thinly perceptible outer layer, gelatinous and elastic, a swirl of images folding upon itself inside me—trees, limbs, blood, bicycle, two men—a spinning tornado of nightmare scenes, like the vortex in *The Wizard of Oz*—pieces of a broken home, a cow, a witch on a bike, spinning into the darkened sky.

And because I felt so stirred up, I felt almost incapable of keeping my story to myself. I wanted to talk, to tell others, friends I hadn't told, my in-laws. And to the ones I had told, I wanted to tell more. For years, I had spared telling others my story, partly because I didn't know the whole story and partly because it felt too terrifying to tell. I chose my listeners carefully, requiring that friends earn my trust and make me feel safe before I let them into the storm.

I chose the moments to tell them the story even more carefully, plotting for a time when we would be alone, when we would have time to sit, to soak, to be humble. One time in high school, I sat under the night sky and told the story to a girl I had a crush on, watching her face slacken and eyes well. In that moment, I felt both close and guilty—guilty that I was enjoying feeling close to her; that I had somehow used my brother's story to win her affection.

But now there was no editing, no restraint. I cried with my wife as we sat in our apartment and relived the horror. I ordered beer after beer at a bar in the East Village, as I told a friend for what purpose the killers had used their knife. I sat around the white Formica table in the kitchen of my in-laws in New Jersey and recounted everything, taking pleasure in rendering them silent. I wanted the world to quiet. I wanted the world to stop. I wanted people to stop what they were doing, to hang up their phones, to put down their forks, to turn off their TVs, to log off the internet, and listen.

I wanted them to see the evil my brother had seen, I wanted them to feel the grip of the hands around their necks, I wanted them to feel afraid, I wanted them to be humble, I wanted them to admit that life was not orderly, that endings weren't always happy. I wanted them to live without denial, without darkness, without dissociation. It was almost aggressive on my part, emotionally murderous, violent. I wanted to shatter the sanctity of the worlds around me. I wanted them to feel what I was feeling. I wanted them to feel Jon. I wanted them to feel death. I wanted to feel less alone.

In my small home office, I sat at my desk and tried to write the statement that I would read at the parole hearing. It came in fits and spurts. Andy had been doing research, and been advised that we should describe our suffering. We should talk about how the murder affected us, how it debilitated us, how we experienced this loss. It was the ultimate writing assignment, and I felt like I was failing. I thought about the person who'd written the police report: how dispassionately he told the story of Jon's death; how he asked all the right questions and noted the answers dutifully on his page. I was nothing compared with him. I was not that writer. That writer had the courage to face and report the facts. I could not face anything.

I began to see the color red everywhere I looked. Not a hallucination but a reminder of Jon. I thought about how my mother had once told me that she decorated each of our bedrooms in colors that expressed our personalities. My room was blue. Andy's was brown. Jon's was red, red like the color of his hair, red like his bike. Red, I thought now, like his blood.

I began keeping a journal in a red notebook, writing only with a red pen. I saw redheads walking the street. One night, with the hopes of distraction, I went to Brooklyn's Prospect Park to see a performance of Spalding Gray, the monologist, but red followed me there. Spalding usually told his own stories, but on this night, he was going to take some selected audience members onstage and interview them about theirs.

The first interviewee was a clean-cut guy in his thirties whom Spalding had chosen because he had seen the man eating a protein bar called Smart. Spalding was fascinated by this product's name and assumed that it somehow made its consumer more interesting. It didn't. The guy didn't have much to say beyond his one- or two-word answers, and Spalding, and the audience, shifted in their seats. The next person was even less memorable, and Spalding seemed restless.

Then he called his final interviewee on stage. With each person, the overhead lights shifted color, and this time they bathed the band shell in red. A small boy bounded onstage and took a chair opposite Spalding, who asked his age. "Eleven," the boy replied—the age of my brother. Spalding asked him a few questions about life at his age, and all I could think of was Jon. This is what Jon was like. This age. This brain. This consciousness. And then Spalding asked him one last question: "What do you think happens when you die?" Whatever the boy's answer was, I wouldn't recall, but I would remember that when he gave it, everything was red.

27

PRIOR TO the hearing, Andy and I learned that despite the high-profile nature of this case, the state attorney's office didn't even know that Tillman was up for parole. When Andy spoke with the lawyer down there, the lawyer couldn't believe the news and was disgusted that this had somehow fallen through the cracks. People began coming out of the woodwork and retirement to help us prepare: deputies, lawyers, a representative from the state attorney's office.

The media found out and reported with astonishment how Tillman could possibly be up for parole. Reporters tracked down my parents. Andy, too. The spotlight was back on and, with it, our irrational fear. To protect our privacy, Andy and I wore hats low down over our faces when we got off the plane in Orlando, Florida.

But we were not in this alone. The police and investigators were right there by our side. They, too, were caught by surprise that Tillman was even eligible for release. At our hotel the night before the hearing, Andy and I met with Captain James Walker, a compassionate older man who'd worked with Sheriff's Major Walter Heinrich on the investigation following Jon's murder. "Heinrich called me into his office," Walker recalled later, "and said he wanted me to go over and represent him, and I said, 'It's been a long time; I'm going to need to get the reports.' He said, 'Go get them all.' "

He told us that Jon's murder was the most horrible case he and his colleagues worked on in the history of their department. They had never been involved with anything so brutal. "Was there anything else you wanted to know?" he asked.

"Yes," I said. I told him how I remembered, as a kid, giving a deposition to a cop about what Jon was wearing and how I had asked him to go to the store to get me the candy. I told him how my father insisted years later that that wasn't the case; that *he* was the last to have seen him. Walker's eyes looked sympathetically at mine. "No," he said, "you're right." I had given a deposition that week, he recalled, in which I described standing with Jon on the sidewalk before he rode off into the woods.

My mind reeled, and the next question came without my even thinking about it. "What about the candy?" I asked. "We heard that they found it in Witt's trailer."

"Yes," he said, "Witt had given it to his son."

It took a few moments for this to sink in. I had been on the sidewalk. I *had* had that conversation with Jon. He had gotten me the candy. Witt had killed him and taken it. And given it to his son? He had a son? He gave my brother's candy to him? The candy of the boy he had just killed?

It was too much, too real, too terrible. At once, I felt connected and disconnected, heartened by the fact that my memory had not been a lie, but disgusted at the new knowledge I had obtained. I was angry. Furious. Vengeful. I was so caught up in my emotions that I barely heard the deputy when he said he had a question for us. He wanted to know how dramatic we wanted him to be at the parole hearing the next day. Plenty, we said; we wanted to do whatever we could to keep this guy in prison. The deputy reached into a gym bag and pulled out a large, heavy metal rod—the exact kind of drill bit that Tillman had used to strike my brother. He said that, during his statement, he could take out the drill bit and crash it on the table to show the parole board what Jon had endured. We told him to go for it.

Andy and I returned to our hotel room and stayed up late talking about what we had learned, going over our speeches for the next day. At one point, the room was dark and Andy was sleeping, but I still felt awake. I looked over and saw the closet door open, and the blur of two people running inside it: Jon and Tillman. I couldn't move, couldn't scream, could only feel some invisible force pulling at my feet, the blanket peeling off of me as I floated off the bed toward the darkness of the closet, midair, shutting my eyes. When I opened my eyes, I realized I had been dreaming. The closet door was shut. The darkness was gone.

The next morning, we woke to newspaper headlines about the hearing. The hearing had brought back the coverage, and memories for those who had worked on the case. "The way some longtime residents remember it," wrote the *St. Petersburg Times*, "the murder of 11-year-old Jonathan Kushner was when Tampa seemed to lose its small-town innocence." Heinrich, now retired, told the reporter, "We've had some other major cases, but I think in this particular case the emotions of the community were unbelievable." He went on, "I guess I've seen so much of it over the years. But I think I got caught up in the emotion of this one. There's only a few cases where that happened to me. He was so innocent, you know?"

The room of the parole hearing was packed. A camera crew was set up with lights. It was hard enough for Andy and me to have to make our statements at all, let alone while being filmed for the evening news. I asked a reporter if he could please not film us. He said his boss wouldn't let him get away with that. But maybe he could just shoot us from behind, showing only the backs of our heads.

We listened to the testimony of Tillman's mother and brother. They didn't have much to say beyond that Tillman was working hard on his studies, and they hoped the parole commission would let him out. Their attorney followed by recounting all the rehabilitation programs that Tillman had been involved with, how he had gotten good grades in prison classes. He was leading a Bible study group. He was studying to get some kind of degree and had gotten good grades.

Prior to the hearing, Andy had discussed the order of our presentations with Walker, so that we would have maximum impact. It was decided that Walker would go first, mapping out the crime and the case against Tillman, followed by Andy, then me, and, finally, the prosecutor. Walker stood beside us and addressed the court, calling the case "the most brutal and sadistic homicide of a child that I have ever been assigned to." He recounted the abduction, the attack. When he got to the part about the drill bit they had hit Jon with, he held up the long metal rod as the room looked on in horror—and then he slammed it on the table for emphasis. He also noted that, months after incarceration, he was transporting Tillman along with a lieutenant when the prisoner told him he had a list of people he wanted to kill, including the assistant state attorney at the time, a detective on the case, a chaplain, his attorney, and a sergeant in the jail. "Eleven-year-old, eighty-five-pound Jonathan Kushner didn't get a chance at life because of Gary Tillman's brutal and sadistic acts," Walker concluded, saying that Tillman should never be released.

I watched Andy next, leaning forward toward the microphone on the table as he held his speech in his hands. Andy and I had always been best friends, and going through this experience together had brought us even closer. Our experiences with Jon's murder were so different—given our own personalities and our difference in ages at the time of his death—but we were united in our grief, and anger.

"For over ten years, I completely shut down and barely talked about it with anyone, including my own parents," he said. "It was terrible going through my biggest growing years holding down, pushing down, such a deep, dark, horrible secret. Although I have since gotten lots of help, I am scarred for life. To this day, I struggle with many complicated issues. I hate knowing, with every fiber of my being, that the worst possible nightmare really can come true at any moment for me or any of the people I love.

"One of my favorite moments, though, is at night when my own child sits on my lap in a rocking chair with a little white stuffed dog, and together we listen and sing to a couple of songs. And then we give each other a big hug, a kiss, and I tuck them into bed. I look into my child's sweet, innocent eyes, and almost every time, a shudder goes tearing through me. How will I ever bear to let my children out into a world that I know can and has been so horrible and dangerous, where someone like Tillman can be waiting? What am I going to do when it's their turn to have a bike and ride it on their own?

". . . Jon never got to be tucked in bed again or hugged and kissed. I don't get to watch with pride as he grows up. I don't get to have our relationship continue to build like it has between my other brother and me. Every holiday picture on my walls, since 1973, is missing a brother, someone's uncle, cousin, son, friend. I struggle to remember my little brother, Jon, in some of the sweet ways I described earlier, but it is so hard, because what I mostly see, in my mind, is him struggling helplessly against two strong grown men and being murdered and mutilated. I was only thirteen at the time, and for twenty-four years, I have suffered intensely and will continue to suffer for the rest of my life, as will my parents and brother and many close people around me.

"I cannot bear the thought that Tillman, this man who intentionally brutally murdered and horribly mutilated my little, barely eleven-year-old, brother might someday be released and allowed to live out a normal life with you, me, and the rest of society."

Then it came to me. I had been through several drafts of a statement. Though Andy and I had been advised by a psychologist to speak about our own suffering—as a way to personalize our case and create more emotional impact—I felt uncomfortable drawing attention to myself this way. But I also wanted to do whatever I could to keep Tillman from being paroled. Underneath the table and away from view, I held Jon's lucky red rabbit foot in my hand.

"I'd like to show you a picture from 1970," I began. I passed an old black-and-white photo up to the parole board. It was a picture of Jon, Andy, and me sitting in front of our family fireplace. I was between them with a huge smile on my face, my arms around each of them, pulling them close while they—visibly annoyed at my uncool display of affection—tried to slip free. "On the left is my older brother, who's here with me today," I said through my tears. "I'm in the middle; on the right is Jon, my other older brother, my other best friend.

"Jon was extraordinarily playful and loving. He was a dream to me, taking me under his wing, inventing new games every day. He loved going to camp. He was creative and did hilarious Donald Duck impressions. He worked hard to overcome a learning disability and was making great progress. He loved riding his bike. On his eleventh birthday, he got a big new green bike from my parents. Six weeks later, for a reason we'll never know, he took his old red bike for one last ride into the woods to get me and him our favorite candies at 7-Eleven.

"Although I am sincerely grateful for the opportunity to speak here today, I am physically sickened by this experience. It disgusts me that I or anyone should have to explain why this savage who murdered and sexually mutilated my sweet, helpless brother should not be granted parole.

"Everyone who has been touched by this tragedy—the community, the law enforcers, the investigators, the friends and family—has suffered. It is impossible to express the depth of pain and loss my family and I have experienced. I suffer because of the terrifying week we had to endure while Jon was missing, because of the horror of how his body was desecrated after he died—and the fact that these sadists had intended to torture him while he was alive. I suffer from the vulnerability of walking around like an open wound, from fear, often irrational, for myself and my loved ones. Most of all, I suffer every day because I am without Jon. I cannot watch him grow up. I cannot share my life. I miss him.

"Though I know I will never hold my brother again, I have

had some peace of mind knowing that one of his murderers has been executed and the other is spending his life in prison. I never imagined that Gary Tillman could actually be considered for parole. I appreciate and respect your roles as commissioners, but I also appeal to you as brothers, sisters, children, and parents. Would you want your child riding a bike while this murderer takes a stroll through the park? No one should have to suffer even a moment of fear as a result of this hearing. Twenty-four years ago, the sanctity of the people of Tampa was shattered by this case; they will surely know if that happens again this morning.

"As you are aware, if Tillman were to commit the same crime today, he would not even be eligible for parole. Florida now has a law that, thankfully, protects us. The only reason we are here is because he beat the clock when he staked out, attacked, murdered, and sexually mutilated an eleven-year-old boy. For the sake of society, my family, and my dead brother, Gary Tillman should not benefit from his good timing. He does not deserve one day of freedom for the lifetime he brutally denied Jon."

Finally, the representative from the state's attorney's office spoke last—and summed up the case against Tillman. When he recapped what the defense had said about Tillman's various accomplishments in prison, he concluded by saying, in a booming voice, "So what?!"

It was in the hands of the commission now. Everyone sat silently, looking up at them when Commissioner Maurice Crockett, a middle-aged African American man, removed his glasses, bowed his head, and wiped his eyes. "This has probably been the most difficult case for me to deal with emotionally," he said, looking at Andy and me. "My heart goes out to you."

It was time to set Tillman's release date. With their microphones off, the parole board broke into a discussion. I had no idea what they were talking about; it sounded like legalese. After a few eternal minutes, I could hear them adding up numbers—years, I gathered—that they were tacking onto Tillman's sentence. The numbers were coming at random—three, two, one, four; I couldn't keep track—until finally the state attorney leaned over and whispered, "He's never getting out."

"We're going to need a calculator," Crocket said finally. They began adding up the years. Years for the brutality and heinousness of the crime. Years for the rape and sexual mutilation. Years for trying to hide the crime by burying Jon in the orange grove. Finally, the parole board announced its verdict: Tillman was sentenced to another 102 years in prison, or to the year 2096. He would still be eligible for parole every five years, but those hearings—I was assured later—would be just a formality.

After the hearing, various people came up to Andy and me and expressed their sympathy. They congratulated us for testifying and said how important it is for the families of victims to be present, to say something, to honor the memory of the departed. Someone has to speak for the dead. A huge cop with a crew cut came up to me with tears in his eyes and said that he, too, has to go to parole hearings to speak for his murdered brother. It knocked me out: to connect with this guy at this moment in this place, to connect with all these people around me who rallied together on my brother's behalf, just as the people of Tampa had joined hands to search the woods by the 7-Eleven.

Outside the courtroom, we called our parents and told them the news. I don't remember what was said, other than sharing a tremendous sense of relief among the four of us. But for me, the story wasn't done. I wanted more. More connection. More details. There was still so much I didn't know. The rest of the story. I wanted to know everything I had never known before: I wanted to know more about my brother's killers. Why had they done this? How exactly did they get caught? What really happened during that week when Jon was missing? How did the community face the ultimate nightmare? How did my parents survive? I also wanted to know something that I had always been too overwhelmed to find out: Who was Jon when he was alive?

I wanted the reality to be more real, more complete, convinced that the more I knew, the more complete I would feel too, and the more I would be connected with my family—with Jon. Maybe this was some fundamental nature of life; something that applied to everyone. Maybe we can't feel complete until we know enough to tell our stories. But learning our stories isn't something we can do alone.

28

THE FEAR first hit at a carnival. It was 2002, and I was in Davis, California, visiting family friends with my wife and my two kids, a three-year-old and a newborn. We were riding the wild carousel of early parenthood: the donkey rides and cotton candy, the face painting and sand art. Our friends had young kids too, born around the same time as ours and raised for a few years down the block in Brooklyn until they moved out west. We had known them since we were teenagers, and marveled at our new roles as moms and dads. Life had transformed from dive bars and Dead shows to Chuck E. Cheese's and the Wiggles.

On one hand, it was incredible pressure—the feeling of having to provide and care for these little human beings, to make money, to make a home, to keep them alive and clean in the storm of mayhem and meltdowns. But we embraced the joyful chaos. As we pushed our overstuffed strollers around the suburban fair, sticky sippy cups and ragged baby dolls spilling from our arms, we did so with the harried insanity and good-humored amazement that every new parent knows. I wanted my kids to have the same sense of freedom and adventure that my parents had given me, despite the nightmare of Jon's murder, and I didn't ever want to stand in the way.

But, as I learned in a flash that afternoon, the freedom comes with fear, too. All of a sudden I realized that my three-year-old wasn't beside me. I asked my wife where she was, and she didn't know either. Panic shot through my veins, a kind of paralytic seizure that immobilized my body and mind. *Where is my kid?* The crowd seemed to thicken around me, the people replicating in numbers to obstruct my view and block my path.

The fear turned to adrenaline as I pushed my way through the families and called my child's name. As my feet quickened and my words became louder, the fear grew, enveloping me and distorting the surroundings. The sun grew brighter and rides more blurry. The music turned deafening and the fair grotesque; the man churning kettle corn and the woman twisting balloon dogs completely oblivious to the fact that I couldn't find my little girl. Time slowed terrifyingly, the carousel of joy just a moment before grinding down to a halt. *Where is she?*

As I shouted her name, I could see the faces of other parents turning toward mine in slow motion, the slow motion of disconnect. This wasn't happening, was it? Could it happen again? A stranger snatching my child, just as strangers had snatched my brother. The sanctity of statistics had long been a comfort for me in my own life, the near-impossible likelihood that what had happened to Jon could happen to me or my brother. But now it felt like it was happening again. With each leap, it didn't even feel like something I was imagining, it felt like something real. My daughter was gone. She was gone. Gone forever. Taken. Whisked away. In the back of a car, a truck—I had no idea—but I knew it. I was convinced. She was gone. It was happening. This was real.

In the panic, I caught a glimpse of my wife's stricken face; she felt it too. She hadn't even been through what I had been through in my life, but by marrying me, she was a part of it now. She was a trauma victim, turned inside out from the knowledge that the ultimate nightmare is real, that it can happen, that it does happen, that it happened to my family, to my parents, to me—and now to her. For so long, she had felt like an interloper, like the horror was not hers, like she didn't have the right to share the shock, the fear, the grief. But she did. And, I soon realized, she was suffering from the same plague of silence that had isolated me. She had been selective in whom she told about Jon's death, just as I had been. But by doing this, she felt estranged from her peers, unable to have the other moms understand just why she might have felt more hesitant to let her kid out of her sight than they did. But she had every right to feel and own her pain. Trauma is a virus, and it infects the people who love you. It is intergenerational. She loved me, and she was traumatized, just as, I knew, my own children would experience their own unique experience of their uncle's death too.

Finally, that day at the fair, I caught sight of my girl. She was with her friend by the pony ride, oblivious, smiling, laughing. She must have just run off for a moment, despite knowing better. Then she got separated, drawn perhaps by the sound of the other children riding on the animals' backs. The fear that had so devoured me in the last few minutes gave way to a rush of relief, a cascade of warmth flooding the cold inside me as I ran up to her and lifted her in my arms and said, "Where were you? What happened? Where'd you go?"

She had no idea why her father was acting this way, why he seemed so scared and so strange, why his face had this look of devastation, this weird mix of distress and release. And as I held her, I talked myself down as best I could. I told her never to run off like that again, to always stay beside us, to be careful in crowds, not to dash off without us knowing. And for a moment, she looked into my eyes and said, "Okay, Daddy, I won't."

Then she pointed to the ponies and asked if she could have a ride. And I was reaching into my pocket, taking out some cash, handing it to the man with the reins. And then I was standing there with my wife, still shaken, as we watched our daughter ride in circles on the pony. We saw the way she was delighting in the feeling of motion, the strong animal carrying her around, the country music on the radio, the smell of cotton candy, the freedom of the moment and the feeling of life.

29

DESPITE EVERYTHING I had learned over the years about Jon's murder—even the details about the crime and candy from the parole hearing—the resolution that I hoped would come with such knowledge was still eluding me. The reality of Jon's death, and perhaps the reality of death itself, remained incomplete. The fear was alive. I had children now, and I would have to find a way to stay sane, to remain functional, to not let the fear of death and, more particularly, the fear of abduction, overwhelm the freedom I wanted them to experience in life. I could see already that I was not alone in this struggle. My friends were going through the conflict too. Kids were not going off on their own like we did when we were young, not even the older kids.

The culture had changed. CNN broadcast news stories of missing kids. We heard about Amber Alerts, followed drawn-out abduction stories on *Nancy Grace*. The stories were flying across the internet too. Of course, this wasn't to say that parents had no reason to be mindful. But at what point does fear subsume mindfulness? Parents, drunk on the fear, began hovering over their kids. Psychologists had coined a term: helicopter parents. Instead of letting the kids run free, free time became regimented. Suddenly there were playdates, and play had to be scheduled like dentist appointments. Instead of heading out the door and running off for hours, kids were shuttled around by their parents. Instead of playing basketball up the street, they were signed up for a relentless crush of after-school activities.

When kids weren't enrolled at some after-school activity, they were home on their computers or playing video games. The personal computer revolution swept the country, providing a new source of leisure and entertainment—a convenient new phenomenon for parents who were more comfortable having their kids indoors. There was nothing wrong or corrupting about the new technology: it was just a tool that parents employed to make their lives easier.

For kids, it felt like a secret world inaccessible to grown-ups, a digital tree house all their own. The Web was their new secret woods, and they were fleeing there. But the promise of new adventures online carried the same old fears. The more time young people spent on the net, the more parents and pundits worried about child predators lurking there. This just seemed like a new means for a kidnapper to lure and kill kids. Once again, the perceived threat overwhelmed the rarity of the reality. Kids were more likely to die from an accident inside the house than get murdered by a kidnapper. But the reality of statistics didn't matter. We had gone from a generation of freedom to a generation of fear.

At the same time, there were more, and beneficial, precautions in place. Unlike when we were kids, teenagers now knew about AIDS and other STDs. The drinking age was now higher in most states. Driver's licenses couldn't be altered into fake IDs as easily as when we were young. But despite all this, the fear still lived in me. I had spent a lifetime not knowing the whole story of what happened to my brother that October day in 1973. The less I had known, the more the specter of his murder had grown.

This was partly because I was afraid to ask the questions and partly because I didn't know which questions to ask. But I was different now. I had been working as a journalist for years. I knew how to report and re-create a story, how to dig up facts and bring the past back to life. I realized that I could use my reporting skills to dig up my brother's story like I had never done before. I could talk with people, research the case, discover all the missing pieces, and put them back together once and for all.

Something inside of me needed to know the full story so well that I could tell it myself. Perhaps I wanted to do this so I had a sense of control, of understanding. Or perhaps I just thought that by bearing witness, I could feel closer to Jon and somehow make the feelings of panic go away. I just didn't know how to go about this, what I would do, how I would do it, what I would say. The fact was, I just wasn't ready at the time. I didn't know why, or really question it. But eight years later, the moment would come, and it took the experience of death to get me started.

30

"WHAT HAPPENED to the truck that was in front of us?" It was February 2010 when my father, now seventy-six, asked me this question. His beard had become short and gray, a black beret over his wavy gray hair, his brown eyes blinking calmly behind his round-framed glasses. He was sitting next to me in the passenger seat of my car as I was driving to give a lecture on one of my books. A large truck had been driving in front of us, and now my dad wondered what had happened to it, as if it had suddenly vanished into thin air. In fact, the truck had pulled away from us a half hour before, but he was just aware of it now.

There was a reason for his strangely delayed reaction. For the past eight years, he had been fighting cancer, which had recently spread from his lungs to his brain. The brain tumor was degrading his memory, and he seemed to be forgetting more and more. My father wasn't a fearful person—something I always found remarkable given Jon's murder—but losing his faculties was something he long seemed to dread. "If I can't read anymore," he once told me, "I wouldn't want to live."

Losing my parents was something I'd obsessed about as long as I could remember. I seemed to fear it more than my friends worried about their own moms and dads. Perhaps it was Jon's death that left me this way. But I always had a heightened vulnerability that my parents could be gone at any second. This manifested in those paranoid visions and moments, like when I convinced myself that one of them was in a passing ambulance or had been murdered by strangers.

With my dad's cancer, that fear became more real and pronounced, a ticking bomb that sounded nearly every day. Not only was I afraid of losing my father—a man who in addition to raising me was also a close friend and inspiration—but also I was afraid of losing another connection to Jon. Because I had so few memories of my brother, I looked to my dad, my mom, and Andy as repositories of the past. They could remember the brother who eluded me, hear his voice, recall his touch. When people die, they live on in the ones who knew them, and I needed my family to help Jon live on inside me.

The problem was that I long feared talking about Jon with them. It felt too painful, too frightening, too selfish. I was still overprotective, scared to upset them by asking them to recall their dead son and brother. I'm sure this wasn't entirely altruistic, though. By not talking with them about Jon, I didn't have to feel my brother's presence myself or feel the horror of his demise. But the older I got—the older they got—the more I had a sense that my time was running out. When my father died, a piece of Jon would die with him.

And so, often before I saw my father, I had the same conversation with myself: *Talk to Dad about Jon*, I'd think. *Take out a tape recorder. Have him tell you the story.* But then I would see him, and I wouldn't say anything about it. I would just give myself over to the flow of our time together—talking about my kids, the Bucs, my writing, his retirement, hanging out, eating, laughing, enjoying our walks—and then I'd be gone.

Now, however, I had the terrible feeling that I had already lost some of my dad, even though he was still alive. His mind was going. A tumor was growing inside, pushing away his memories, or whatever was left of them. He couldn't even remember when the truck in front of us had driven away; how was he going to remember the story of Jon?

Though I still couldn't muster the courage to ask him to do this, I did want to make sure that he knew of my intention to write about Jon someday. I wanted his blessing, his okay that I wasn't somehow exploiting myself or my family by telling our story. This wasn't the first time, though, that we had this conversation. I had first mentioned it years before. After the publication of my first book, *Masters of Doom*, in 2003, I began thinking seriously about writing about Jon one day, and sat down with my parents to discuss this with them.

They were, as I expected them to be, completely supportive. This was consistent with how they had led their lives, founding the grief support groups in Tampa, and becoming so active in the grief support community. My parents weren't perfect, but they were talkers and thinkers and feelers, despite the fact that talking and thinking and feeling about Jon was often too painful to occur inside our own home. My dad had taken both a personal and anthropological interest in death and dying, lining his office shelves with books on the subject. When he donated his massive library upon his retirement, the couple dozen books he kept were the ones about death.

"Wow, what a heavy, heavy task you've laid out for yourself," he wrote me in an email after we first talked about my writing a book on Jon, "but it will also be an enlightening one, in the sense that it will make you lighter and even wiser than you are now at the same time. And if you're looking for books to read, we have some . . . whatever, you have, as you know, made a very large decision, and I wish you well on your journey. I think you and I will find that my memory about lots of things is lacking. This may be a pattern with me. You know how I remember so little from my boyhood . . . the shrink suggested I blocked out much of my first 10 years or so because that was my response to my father's death when I was 9 1/2. I may well have done the same with Jon. We'll see . . . anyway, godspeed."

Other emails followed, more recommendations for books to read, such as *Hour of Gold, Hour of Lead*, the diaries and letters of Anne Morrow Lindbergh, wife of famed aviator Charles Lindbergh, about the kidnapping and murder of their baby Charles Jr. in 1932. "Lindbergh said, actually, that suffering alone doesn't make for wisdom," Dad wrote. He often used ellipses in his emails, as if to indicate his stream of thought. "One has to remain vulnerable . . . open . . . to more suffering . . . and to more love . . . it's rather wonderful, as I recall." He referenced a portion of the book where Lindbergh attributes her survival to the support she received from others, how she said, as my dad put it, "you gotta have at least one person whom you love and who loves you, and talk to that person and be supported by that person."

Later, one day when we were standing on the sidewalk in front of the house in Tampa—the same sidewalk where I thought I had last seen Jon—my father told me, “It will be the best thing you ever write.” As reassuring as this was to hear, something in his words unsettled me. Despite everything I told him, I wasn’t resolved about writing about Jon yet, not completely. I still hadn’t even mustered the strength to discuss Jon with him beyond this cursory idea. My father was just trying to lend me his support by giving me this encouragement but, in a way, it felt like a burden, an assignment from a professor that I didn’t want to complete.

Several years later, during the drive to New York, I broached the topic again, talking of my intention to write the book one day. But this time was different. Inside me, I felt an inevitability, that if I did ever write the story, it would happen after my father was gone, and that I would have to live with the reality that the conversations I long feared of having with him might not even be an option. Maybe he knew this too, but as we went down the highway, he told me again how much he supported my pursuit. Perhaps, somehow, I would be completing work for the both of us.

31

On Memorial Day weekend 2010, I was with my father at hospice when he died. My mother, wife, and kids happened to all be there, too, when the moment came. To watch someone die, let alone my own father, was something I never imagined, and the reality was beyond anything I had experienced before.

As frightening as it felt to hear his breathing change and see the blueness crawl from his fingertips over his body, it felt like a privilege to be there with him, to share his last seconds, to make sure he wasn't alone. My father had lived with death for so long, from the death of his father to the death of his son. He had read about it, studied it, joked darkly about it, and I was grateful to be there with him when it was his time. When his last breath left his body, it was remarkable to see that it was just a body he'd left behind. It was my father, but it wasn't my father. It didn't feel scary to me anymore, it just felt like he was gone, like there really was some ineffable essence that had escaped, and that the body was no longer his.

But then an even more unexpected series of events was set in motion, as we got swept up in the ceremonies and rituals following his death. Suddenly our family was the focus of grieving again, something that had not happened since Jon was killed. This wasn't something stated explicitly, but it was felt. And, for me, it felt so cyclical. There I was in the synagogue, forty-two years old, just about the age my father was when he lost his own son, and I was surrounded by many of the same people who had come there in 1973 for Jon's memorial service.

We hugged in the lobby, where the banners honoring my brother still hung. I stood beneath the one dedicated to me as my kid took a picture. My hair was long, my face unshaved, a torn black ribbon on my suit. The custom at a Jewish memorial service is that the family is led in last after everyone has taken his or her seats, and this is what we did as well. My brother told me that the last time he had done this was for Jon, and how awkward it felt to have the eyes of the congregation upon us.

I couldn't recall that moment, but now, as I walked down the aisle, I felt a sense of comfort, a feeling that these people had been there for my family during the horror thirty-seven years earlier, just as they were there for us now. When it came time for my eulogy, I walked up the same steps to the bimah where I had bar mitzvahed years before. Now I was there to honor my father, as his casket sat closed before us.

As I looked out on all the familiar faces from different stages of my life, I spoke of my love for my father and his profound influence on me. I also shared the struggle I'd long had over a fundamental question: "How do we survive the death of someone we love?" I said, "How would I survive losing him?" But, I went on, I had recently found something of an answer. It had happened late one night not long ago after I had returned to my parents' house from visiting my dad in the hospital. I was having trouble sleeping in his office, under his shelves heavy with books on death and dying, his walls decorated with the stuff from his life: the Mr. Natural postcard I'd sent him from college; the black-and-white photos of his father leading a construction site in Palestine; the mouse pad with a picture of his grandchildren.

There between two thick and dusty books, I found a copy of a book proposal he had written about twenty-five years before. It was for what I remembered him calling his "book on suffering." The proposal described how my dad, after Jon's death, began to study how other people suffer from loss and death. But what began as a kind of "self-therapy," as my dad put it, evolved into an anthropology book he wanted to write on "the development and characteristics of individuals and peoples who have transformed the experience of suffering into positive approaches to surviving."

My father never got around to writing the book. But, in a way that I'm sure would have deeply moved him, reading the yellowed pages of the proposal that night fulfilled something profound in me. As I told the mourners gathered with our family, it gave me a way of thinking and feeling about death, including his, that would help to support me in the many long nights to come.

"The observation that all relationships (including that with ourselves) end in separation and loss is almost banal," my father wrote, "yet, it is important because it is a universal in human experience. Moreover, other kinds and degrees of loss threatening personal and cultural identity are common in life cycles of individuals and cultures. Often, there is, in literature, the suggestion that some, through means that are as yet unclear, make use of the experience of suffering to enhance growth, to heighten awareness and appreciation of the good and the joyous experiences that are also part of human life. In his discussion of the sacrifice of Isaac, the first survivor, Elie Wiesel points out that Yitzhak means 'he who will laugh,' that Isaac transformed his suffering, that he remained capable of laughter, and that 'in spite of everything, he did laugh.' "

32

SOON WE WERE in the back of a town car, heading to the cemetery where my father would be laid to rest. We were short a pallbearer, and at the last second, I saw a familiar man being ushered over by my brother. It was Arnie Levine, the family friend and lawyer who had been so instrumental in helping us through Jon's case. As we walked slowly over the stony path to the gravesite, I thought how appropriate it was that Arnie was there carrying my father, just as he had carried him through such a hard time so long ago.

As we came to the site, I saw the marker for Jon's grave, the grave that was empty, since his ashes had been spread in the bay. But it was there, a reminder for me and everyone else of what had happened, and I'm sure it was on everyone's mind as the rabbi began his prayers. Something was happening, something I could feel: Jon's presence coming back along with my dad's.

This wasn't just something in my imagination. Reporters began calling the house, gathering information for a few stories on my father. Invariably, they brought up the story of my brother, asking me how my father got through the tragedy. Some of the reporters had been at our house during the week that Jon was missing, and the memories came flooding back. A story ran in the *St. Petersburg Times*, along with a photo of my parents from 1973, sitting on their couch and waiting anxiously for news on their still-missing son.

Daniel Ruth, the columnist, wrote about the awkwardness he'd felt when assigned to interview my parents after the discovery of Jon's murder, and how, to his surprise, my father reacted when he saw him at the memorial service soon after: "Gilbert Kushner walked over to me, shook my hand and invited me to join his family inside the synagogue for the funeral service. At the very nadir of this man's greatest personal tragedy, he graciously wanted me to know he wasn't offended" by Ruth's reporting. Ruth headlined his tribute to my father "A Man of Uncommon Grace and Courage."

And the experience still lingered for Ruth, just as it did for me and the others. "Since 1973, I have probably driven up and down that stretch of [road near my parents' house] thousands of times," he went on. "I am always reminded of what happened there. A little boy rode his bike to the store and never came home. And now with the passing of this man of uncommon grace and courage, in a sense a little boy has at last been reunited with his father—Jonathan Kushner has come home."

How fitting it was, I thought, that all these memories were coming back around Memorial Day weekend. It felt as if something larger was at play, something that defied my usual skepticism, a sense that a story was unfolding around me. Throughout the week, we gathered at my parents' house for shiva, the mourning period when visitors come to the home of the deceased's family to say Kaddish, the memorial prayer. Every time the front door opened, I watched someone else come inside carrying his or her memories, the memory of having been in this house decades before during the shiva for Jon.

People approached me quietly, telling me as much, how they had been here at that time. They recalled how awful and surreal the week felt, how they watched in awe as my parents moved among them, lending their support to people who were coming for them. With each conversation, I felt the past coming to life. I spoke with Cindy Silverman, the speech therapist who had worked with Jon during his difficulties in school. For my entire life, I had been told that Jon had a learning disability, that he was slow, but Cindy explained that this wasn't the case: he suffered from an auditory deficit disorder, which had nothing to do with his intelligence.

The more I heard from people, the more I wanted to know. I saw an older Jewish man sitting on the couch by himself, and we got to talking. He was Stan Rosenberg, who'd helped lead the search party throughout the week for my brother, and had combed the woods himself. I spoke with his wife, Madelyn, who helped feed the volunteers along with dozens of other local women. I spoke with Arnie and his wife, Gail, about their support that week, and the efforts to find the murderers. And I spoke with other family and friends, not just about the horror of the week that Jon was missing, but the life they recalled leading up to that day.

I began to get dizzy with memories, feeling the feelings of everyone here, hearing their thoughts, their fears, their sadness, their admiration. At one point, I found myself by our piano, talking with a Hassidic Jew, the son of the rabbi at the local Hillel, the Jewish student group for which my father was the university liaison. I asked him what happens now, as far as he was concerned; what happens to you after you die? His eyes met mine compassionately and eagerly. He told me how my father would be buried in the traditional Jewish way, and how, when the messiah comes, all the dead Jews will roll from their graves underground to Jerusalem, where they will come back to life.

Needing time alone, I retired to my dad's office in the corner of the house. I shut the door and sat at his desk under his shelves of books on death and dying. I wanted to feel his presence, to derive some comfort during a time that seemed so overwhelming and uncomfortable to survive. How had he done it? How had he gotten through the deaths that he had experienced? How had he lived knowing that death was everywhere, that murder was real, that you could walk out the door one morning and never come back? I wanted to know everything. I wanted more memories, more knowledge, more reality to help me through this time, through the rest of my life.

Near his desk, I saw a cloth folder stuffed with papers, and reached for it to see what was inside. There were dozens of pages of notes, typed recollections that he had accumulated over the years. My father was meticulous about keeping track of his professional work, his contributions, his bibliography. I leafed through it all, hoping the residue would smudge my skin and impart the sensation of his fingers pressing on the keyboard.

He also had personal notes, little entries about his life during retirement, his joy of cooking, of shopping, of embracing the domestic chores that felt so simple and fulfilling. And then, on one page, I saw something titled "On Grief." From the second I started reading it, I felt like he had left it for me to find this day.

"You *will* get thru this," my father had written, "much as you might *not* want to get thru it from moment to moment right now.

> You will get thru it because you have no choice, really . . . it just happens . . . no matter what you may feel now. There's something built-in that enables most human beings . . . not all, to be sure . . . but most, to get thru this . . . like feeling very tense and tight and getting into a hot tub and finding there is no way *not* to be relaxed in the hot water because the water does wonderful physiological stuff to you and emotionally too that you cannot avoid. It is built-in to enable us to get thru, to enable us, *force* us, to survive, to stay alive. The question then becomes, after you've understood that it *will* be different, less raw, that the death can not be undone, that you will continue to live and that you will return, a different person, to the life other people define as "normal": "What shall I do with the rest of my life?"
>
> 1. the situation is real and will remain so.
> 2. there's nothing you can do about it, nothing at all.
> 3. now what happens to you?
> 4. who do you want to be?

As I sat there holding the paper, I felt like my dad was there with me, talking to me, asking these questions of me now: What happens to you? Who do you want to be? I knew the answers. I knew them then just as I had known them for years. I wanted to be my brother's brother. I wanted to be the writer of his story.

I wanted to harvest the memories of everyone I could, to read everything I hadn't read, to pour over the case file, talk with the cops, talk with Stan, Cindy, Arnie, my mother, Andy, Jon's friends, Jon's teachers. I wanted to dig up the past, with the help of others, and tell this story of freedom and fear, of adventure and loss, of murder and mystery and survival.

I thought about the canon of Holocaust memoirs, of the Jewish idea of bearing witness, of remembering, of telling the stories, in all their horrific detail, so that people remember, so that no one forgets. I thought about Passover, and how for thousands of years, Jews would gather around a table and recite the story of when we were slaves in Egypt, and how the Haggadah, the prayer book for that holiday, uses the plural first person, *we*: when *we* were slaves, it reads; this is the story of us.

I thought about my own children and the world they were in now—how they rarely went outside; rarely rode their bikes. What happened? I wondered. What happened to my generation? How had we been the kids with so much freedom, who then grew up to deny this freedom to our own children? This adventure. This sense of discovery and danger and risk and recovery. The answers were larger than me, but, I realized, by telling the story of our family, the murder, our survival, perhaps I could help others to think about all of this, why this happened, how we got here. And along the way, I could do something that felt at once inevitable and perhaps a bit megalomaniacal. Who did I want to be? my father asked. I wanted to be the memory harvester. I wanted to learn and tell the story, the whole story of everything. I wanted to bring Jon back to life.

Part 4

33

"HE WAS A funny little baby," my mother said about Jon. We were looking at old photo albums. She was showing me pictures of Jon as a newborn, square black-and-white snapshots of him, a tiny bundle of new life, shortly after he was born in Minneapolis in 1962. "The nurses would comb his hair to a point," my mother said with a smile. "They tied his red hair in a bow."

It was November 2011, and we were in the living room of the house where I had grown up: the white-tiled fireplace, the shelves of Wiesel books, the jazz albums lined up beneath the stereo. She was dressed in white and beige, with gray hair now.

It had been over a year since my father had died, and the drive to finally write the book on Jon had become a reality. I had been in Tampa now, interviewing people, poring over research, spending days at the library, IDS, and elsewhere. It wasn't that I sought "closure" by writing the book. That word always troubled me because it suggested that it was possible to somehow end the grieving, to put a stake in something that was always present and evolving.

I sought more understanding and awareness, a fuller sense of how I came to be the person I was, how my family struggled and endured, and, perhaps most of all, a fuller sense of this person who had such a profound influence on my life. A therapist I had been seeing pointed out that I was also writing about how trauma affects a child, something I hadn't really thought about consciously before. It was true that adults seemed to, out of protectiveness, perhaps, almost discount the feelings of young children experiencing trauma, as though before a certain age a person is somehow inoculated from grief and suffering. But as I learned myself, kids feel and remember more than adults might think.

I was interested in how this story transcended me, how, while our experience of death was unique, the experience of grieving, of living with grief, of living with death, was universal. I was isolated by my grief for many reasons—my age, the circumstances, the mystery—but I had come to see how everyone is isolated by grief; how grief sends you spiraling inside yourself and how only you can find a way out. And the way out, as my parents discovered, was by finding support and community in other people.

Part of me regretted that I hadn't pursued this earlier; that I wasn't writing the book while my father was alive and could participate. But things happen in life when the time is right, I believed, and perhaps my starting this book now was my father's final gift to me. Perhaps I had to experience his death, his passing, the gathering of the people at our house for shiva, before I could fully connect and be present to write the book on Jon. Though I longed for my father to be here, to share his memories, I appreciated that he had set me on my way.

My family and friends supported my writing the book, but they would often remark how hard they thought it would be for me to pursue. I never really thought of it as so foreboding, though. To me, I had lived with the story, the mystery, for so long that I was grateful to have the opportunity to do this at all. While some of the woods where Jon disappeared remained, the specific path he went down was long gone, along with the 7-Eleven. But I would be, figuratively at least, going back down the dark path of the woods now. Going there had always felt like some kind of inevitability, something I would do at some point in my life, and now, I knew, the time had come.

My main concern, really, was for my mother and brother. I had always felt a bit protected by the fact that I was so young when Jon died. My memories of that period were a blur, while, for them, they were fully formed because they were so much older. I felt protective of them and didn't want them to suffer again unnecessarily as I dug the story up again. "Just because I'm going into the woods," I told them, "doesn't mean you have to follow me there." But just as my father had given me his blessing to write the book, my mother and brother were there with me too. And so, with my tape recorder and notebook in hand, I got to work.

Over the years, my mother and I had spoken tentatively about Jon, largely because of my own tentativeness around the subject. But as we sat on the couch leafing through the photos, we could focus on the moment. While we both knew the ending of Jon's story, the fate that awaited him, we could now separate his death from his life, and focus on the life—the sweet life—he had.

Though I knew the contours of my family's story, my mother brought it to life more vividly. I realized that as much as we think we may know about our families, the more questions we ask, the more we learn about ourselves. For days, I sat with my mother and brother in our house, listening to their stories of our family's early life together: the days in the desert, the arrival in Tampa, Jon's struggles. "I always had a worry about him," my mother recalled. "I was not quite sure how he was going to make it. He was very affectionate and very sweet, and I felt protective of him."

I tracked down Jon's former teachers at IDS. One of them, Sandra Parks, the mother of one of Jon's friends, whom I met one day for breakfast, described him as a "gentle soul." She said, "Jonathan was a humble kid; he didn't need to push kids around. Fifth-grade boys would be interested in showing off, but he was not like that."

"He seemed like a gentle person," recalled Jim Bradley, the former principal of IDS, when I phoned him. He was retired out of state. "He wasn't going to hurt anybody else," recalled his wife, Patricia, who also worked at the school. "I do remember that was the feeling: a sweet boy," she said.

John Wing, Parks's son, told me of the time he fell from a tree at IDS, and how Jon was the only kid who stayed around to make sure he was all right. "He said, 'You're okay, just breathe deep,'" Wing recalled. "'You just got the wind knocked out of you.' That was what I remember about Jonathan . . . I thought about that a lot when he was missing; that was the image that I held on to and to this day."

I found Jon's old friends Doug Chisholm and Paul Siddall. They were men now, weathered and aged, but still had sparks of precociousness as they recalled their childhoods with my brother. "Back then parents would say, 'Get out of the house,' and we'd be gone for two or three hours," Chisholm told me. "There was no restrictions," Siddall added. "You had no worries." Even the one alligator rumored to be in the lake, Big George, wasn't a threat. Neither was the trail to the store. "We used to sneak off to go to 7-Eleven," Siddall went on. "We'd go under the bridge and straight down the trail." They'd sneak off during physical education class to go there from school too. "If we wanted to and we weren't supervised we'd go to 7-Eleven and get candy," he said. "By the 7-Eleven, people would dump things," Chisholm said, "like mattresses in the woods."

Parents knew their kids went into the woods, and mine were no different. They didn't worry about abductions. "There was no sense of fear at all," my mother recalled. We had gone through all the albums—the photos of Jon and me playing; of Andy and Jon and me in front of the fireplace; of Jon with the faraway look in his eyes at Andy's bar mitzvah in his wide-collared suit.

I always felt a weird sense of an impending storm as we progressed through the pages, as the year 1973 approached. The closer we got to that time, the more I began to read into the expressions on Jon's face, the look in his eyes, the slackened jaw, the rest of us smiling. My mother saw this too. Perhaps we were reading into everything. Maybe it was just our brains seeking to make sense of what was coming. But we both had the feeling that it was almost as if Jon himself knew that his days were numbered.

The photo album from 1973 went up through the summer, when Jon flew alone to visit his grandparents in Minneapolis. There are photos he shot of the clouds below. Then the photo album stops, and the rest of the pages are blank.

34

On another afternoon in Tampa, I went to the library downtown to look at the microfilm from 1973. The last time I had done that was in junior high, when I spent a week at lunch looking over the articles, trying to piece together the story that I was afraid to discuss at home. As I sat at the microfilm machine now, I felt a different sense of urgency. I wasn't just there reading the stories about the search for Jon and the subsequent case. I was looking at everything—the ads, the football scores, the comics—soaking up the information in an effort to put myself back into the moment, to re-create the times.

Once again, my brain began seeing strange patterns, began making connections in a way that felt almost improper or egocentric. I was not one to think that things were meant to be, that the universe somehow aligned its exterior world to reflect the experiences of individuals. The rain that seemed to always fall on two lovers in a sad scene was just movie rain. And yet, when I looked at the Sunday *Tampa Tribune* that sat on our kitchen table the morning Jon disappeared, I was struck by what I saw.

An article headlined "What Are Our Children Missing?" opened with a quote from a local art teacher and mother of two. "Children today have been shortchanged," she told the reporter. "When I was young, we could wander in the woods, we could breathe and run free."

She and other parents didn't think that life in the early seventies was as adventurous as it seemed. Kids were getting overscheduled, they believed, confined by a regimen of after-school activities that was curtailing their independence and exploration. Children were watching too much television and doing drugs when they should have been adventuring outside, parents lamented. To drive home this point, the article was accompanied by an illustration of a happy, barefoot boy in a straw hat fishing with a line on a broken stick. What kids were missing, the picture implied, was this: wandering in the woods, breathing, and running free.

When parents pine for the good old days, they often pine for the same thing: the days when kids would be playing out in the woods. What was so compelling about this in the first place? Perhaps it was just an extension of the country's pioneering spirit. Kids, boys in particular, seemed expected to be outside with a pocketknife and a fishing pole, fending for themselves in the woods in preparation for their hunting and gathering to come as men.

Mark Twain's Tom Sawyer and Huckleberry Finn roamed the woods along the Mississippi River. So did the kids of the fictional town of Mayberry, North Carolina, on *The Andy Griffith Show*. The woods promised adventure and discovery. Jim Hawkins sailed off to Treasure Island in Robert Louis Stevenson's 1883 adventure novel. The Hardy Boys and Nancy Drew solved crimes in the thickets. The woods held mystery and possibility, secret caves and forts, tree houses and buried fortunes, *Sigmund and the Sea Monsters*. Maybe most important, the woods were where kids could get away from adults.

But as much as kids were encouraged to venture into the woods, parents had their concerns. Fables and fairy tales warned what could happen to wandering kids in enchanted forests. Little Red Riding Hood met the murderous talking wolf; Hansel and Gretel, the child-eating hag. In the *Tampa Tribune* article, parents said that their kids' imaginations were starting to run wild from all the violence on TV. "You should trust your children, and I trust mine," said one parent, "but I'm afraid of what other people might do to them."

The kids who flipped to the comics page in the *Tribune* that morning found strips that, coincidentally, played on these fantasies and fears. In *Barney Google and Snuffy Smith*, Lukey warned Loweezy of trouble in the trees. A "mean ol' wild boar is out yonder in them, an' he's on th' rampage!!" Lukey said. Just below that strip, Archie was telling his dad how he and Jughead found a secret cave in the woods hidden behind bushes by the river. Hearing that the cave was covered in mysterious writings, Archie's dad rejoiced, telling the boys that his paleographic society had spent months searching for "the lost cave tribes," and this must be it. The punch line came when his dad ventured into the cave—only to see that the ancient writing was modern-day spelunker graffiti.

Jon, an Archie fanatic who collected *Archie* comic books, may have read that strip that morning. And if he did, perhaps his mind might have filled with images of the caves that were supposedly hidden in the woods across from our house. The fact that no one had actually found any caves didn't seem to matter, nor did the specter of wild animals in those woods—not boars, but pygmy snakes and water moccasins. The fact was, the majority of parents where we lived, despite what the article said, didn't keep their kids from wandering in the woods at all. Kids were trusted and unleashed, set loose to disappear on their bikes, to breathe and ride free.

That's exactly what Jon intended to do that day. When I spoke with Andy and my mother about that morning, they both recalled it with their own filters of guilt. Andy was still haunted by what would have happened had he not skipped the ride to the synagogue and need Mom to take him. "I had guilt that if I hadn't done that, she wouldn't have gone, and he wouldn't have gone," Andy recalled. "We're looking for a sense of control."

"And blame," my mother said.

"We're trying to bring control—even in a negative, blaming way—to a situation that was out of control."

"And if you had been home," my mother told Andy, "maybe you would have gone with him. There are a lot of what-ifs about what could have happened."

"The ifs are literally infinite," Andy said. "It's so random."

"We all live with it," she said

But there was more to the story that neither of them could tell me, the parts that I, for reasons unique to me, needed to know: the story of Jon's killers, how the community came together, the story of everything. And, after many months of research, reading the court documents, and tracking down family friends, the police, and volunteers, the missing pages I'd been seeking my entire life finally appeared.

35

THE PROBLEMS with Johnny Paul Witt began at the start. Born on January 13, 1943, he grew up a troubled boy. His father, John H. Witt, thought his son showed signs of mental and emotional problems by the age of seven, often "nervous, disturbed, and confused." The boy was placed under psychiatric care. Witt's alcoholic father, however, was part of the problem. According to Johnny's wife, Donna, Witt Senior would tell the boy that "he was no good and would never amount to anything."

Witt's difficulties grew worse when, around age eighteen, he had a head injury during a car crash. Following this accident, his father thought that his son was even more challenging to control. Witt later entered the US Marines, where he was a private first class. But his troubles continued. As a psychiatrist determined later, Witt suffered from "emotional instability reaction, chronic severe; manifested by history of unstable family background and home environment (alcoholic father), difficulties in adapting to figures of authority and school, chronic headaches and feelings of tension and anxiety, and recent impulsive antisocial behavior; predisposition, lifelong history of emotional instability under minimal stress; precipitating stress, routine stress of military duty at the present time." Witt was ultimately deemed unfit for duty and discharged from the marines.

Witt's complications followed him into his marriage at the age of twenty-one to Donna, a woman one year younger who had a two-year-old boy, Troy, from a previous marriage. Donna was prone to depression and felt ignored by Witt. She often wanted to go out, but he wouldn't take her. One night he went to a movie by himself, and she was so upset that she overdosed on aspirin. After having her stomach pumped, Witt had her committed to a mental institution for a few days, a move, she thought, that was done simply to get rid of her—especially when the hospital doctors told her she was fine. "It seemed to me like he wanted me out of the way," she told the police later.

Donna had reason to believe this. She discovered that while she was in the hospital, Witt had been out with her best friend. One night, coming home from a bar with him, Donna confronted him about her jealousy. Witt, who'd been drinking, began choking her. He was now five foot eleven, 155 pounds, with brown hair and blue eyes. Witt grabbed her hands and began squeezing them until they bled. Another time, he got so angry that he drove his fist through the headboard, breaking his thumb.

Witt soon got into the refrigerator repair business with his father, but the pressure of working together often got the better of him. Witt became prone to outbursts around his house, tossing over the kitchen table, and throwing plates and food around the room. Witt would storm out of the house, only to return and claim that he didn't remember his rampage. When Donna, who worked for an answering service, suffered a miscarriage, Witt became even more despondent, as medical bills piled up.

The stress grew worse when Troy, then seven, and another young boy were walking down a sidewalk when Troy darted across the street suddenly and was struck by a car. He was thrown seventy feet before coming to a rest. His shoes were knocked off his feet. The injury was so severe it left him brain damaged with a metal plate in his head. Donna had to quit her job to care for him while he spent several months learning to walk and talk again. I was shocked to read that Troy's accident occurred on October 28, 1971, two years to the day before he and Tillman killed my brother. There was never any indication as to whether this was a motivation for Witt that day, but either way, it filled me with a sense of fear and foreboding.

Witt, who had often spanked his stepson in the past, didn't change his behavior after the accident, according to Donna. One day, Witt came home and told the boy not to wake him if his boss called, then went to sleep. But Troy woke him anyway when the phone rang, and Witt's employer was on the line. Witt grabbed the boy angrily, and, when Donna found out afterward, she berated him. If the metal plate moved in Troy's head, she said, it could kill him. Witt stopped spanking Troy then, but he soon found someone who shared his temperament: Gary Tillman.

With a father who spent two decades in the army and air force, Tillman, as I read in articles and court documents, grew up on the move, shuttling between military bases across the South. Often the new kid in town, Tillman became known as a loner who dreamed of living on a mountaintop as a forest ranger. By ninth grade, his parents noticed that there was something amiss in their son, who "would say things that would maybe not sound right," as his father recalled. "There were other things that just didn't add up to normal thinking." Friends said he had a "keen interest" in poisons, gasses, torture, and other people's suffering.

Tillman was failing classes, lashing out at his father for being too strict, and claiming that he was, as a psychologist noted later, "the king of a secret society." After a childhood friend died, he would regularly march into the woods to play trumpet in tribute to her. In 1971 seventeen-year-old Tillman was diagnosed as a paranoid schizophrenic and briefly institutionalized—until he ran away from the facility. The family continued with outpatient treatment and, later that year, moved to Tampa, where Tillman's father had taken a job as an airline pilot. After graduating high school, Tillman took a menial job at a local shrimp processing plant, where his supervisor found him a slow learner who "seemed uneasy in trying to carry on any other type of conversation" than talking about his favorite hobby: archery.

Tillman soon found someone who shared his passion: Witt, whom he called J.J. They met in 1973 at Tampa Technical Institute, where Tillman was studying drafting and Witt was pursuing electronics. Known around the school as a quiet pair of poor students, the two became friends, and began going hunting together using bow and arrows. Witt enjoyed archery, joining the Gasparilla Bowman's club on a ranch. He went there for tournaments, and began collecting a variety of arrows around the house. They never came home with any game, though. As far as his wife knew, the only thing he shot was an armadillo. The owner of another archery shop frequented by Witt and Tillman told police later that Witt's "hands seemed to be dirty all the time."

One day, Tillman called the Witts and told Donna that his parents were throwing him out of the house. Tillman had left a note on his pillow that morning for his mom and dad. "Since I was asked to leave, I have," he wrote. "You can probably guess where I'm at." Tillman took his calico cat Tiny and began sleeping on the couch at Witt's trailer in Thonotosassa, a rural area north of Tampa.

It didn't take long for Donna, who was now working as a lab technician at Tampa General Hospital, to notice that her husband's young friend displayed odd outbursts. One day Troy accidentally knocked down a model airplane, and a little piece broke off. When Tillman saw this, he picked up the plane and began tearing it into shreds. "Give it to me!" the boy pleaded.

"Any time something of mine is torn up," Tillman said, "I just tear it up." He had done the same thing when the cat knocked over a model car and broke off a wheel. Yet another time, when Donna moved one of Tillman's arrows to a corner, the feather accidentally got mashed down. Tillman picked up the arrow and snapped it in half. He became even more despondent when his cat Tiny was stolen out of his car one day.

Witt was still acting out too. Donna had a black cat that always greeted her at the front door when she came home. One day before going to work, the cat had been jumping at their pet bird, which had flown out of its cage. When Donna came home that day, her cat wasn't there to greet her. Donna began searching around the house, with the help of her son, to no avail. She saw that Witt had left a big foam target in the kitchen, which he had been shooting with his bow and arrows. Donna had a bad feeling and called her husband at work. "John," she said, "where's my cat?"

"I'm sorry, baby," he replied.

"What did you do? Kill it?"

"Yeah." He told her he'd choked the animal and then shot it with an arrow. Donna could still see the bloodstain on the carpet.

Witt seemed to be growing more indifferent to her recently. The couple had gone from having sex almost daily to nothing at all for the past month. Donna didn't know what to make of it. Witt was increasingly introverted and preoccupied. Unbeknown to Donna, Witt and Tillman had hatched a plan: to go, as Tillman put it later, "people hunting." According to the police, "Their prey were human beings."

Witt had killed before, Tillman claimed later, though there was never any evidence to support this. Tillman said Witt had told him that he had killed a man and buried him on a construction site that was later paved over. Witt recalled how the pavement buckled up because of the bloated corpse and needed to be steamrolled back down.

The two drove around town, picking up female hitchhikers—one of whom dove out the window at a red light when she had grown scared. They began heading out to different locations around town, forgetting which they'd been to before, but never found a good victim or didn't have the right opportunity. In mid-October Witt drove to the patch of woods near a 7-Eleven, which was across the way from an archery range they frequented. As he waited in the woods, he saw a young girl playing alone. Witt later told police that he "ran a little girl away from the area I was in; I told her she might get hurt, to leave." Perhaps he feared what he might do to her.

But he returned with Tillman later and told him he thought

it looked like "a good spot to hunt." Shortly after, the two came back to the location, as Tillman recalled later, and parked their car while waiting for a girl to come through the woods. That day, however, they failed to find a girl by herself and, after four hours of frustration, gave up and left. The next week, the week before Jon disappeared, they returned to the 7-Eleven again in Gary's car. "They were stalking for young girls," the police report read, "and again they were disappointed after not being able to have a good opportunity taking one."

But they decided to go back one more time. Sunday morning was Witt's regular day to go hunting and, on Sunday, October 28, he gathered his bow and arrows to shoot on a target range. Witt said he had seen an old, abandoned flat-bottom boat last time he was there, and was hoping he might be able to retrieve it, put some fiberglass back on the boat, and reuse it. Tillman rose from the couch and said he wanted to practice for a turkey shoot that was coming up. Witt agreed to take him along.

That morning, Witt knew that there was usually a work detail at the archery range at this hour, so he pulled up on a riverside trail to hunt cows for a bit until the workers went away. As they were heading through the pasture, however, they heard voices and went to investigate. Spotting a man and his son through the mangroves, they followed quietly behind them, hoping they were on to a deer. To keep their cover, Witt and Tillman slipped into their camouflage outfits, and continued on after them for a bit before growing bored and moving on.

With still more time to kill before the archery range opened, the two drove to another pasture, shot arrows at cans and bottles, and tried to hit a few squirrels. They heard voices again out there, and saw three boys coming across the woods. Witt and Tillman stalked the boys, as the kids dug by the trees looking for rifle bullets from stray hunters. When the boys spotted the two, Witt and Tillman returned to their car.

As they drove off, Witt had the idea to head off to Saint Petersburg, about forty-five minutes away, but he didn't think they had enough gas in the car. So he continued on to the archery range to see if the old boat was still around. When he and Tillman arrived, the bugs were biting them up in force, so they packed up their gear and drove across the street to the 7-Eleven, where, as they discovered, my brother was heading that day.

36

By three o'clock on the afternoon of October 28, I learned, Jon still wasn't back, and the fear began to take hold. My dad went out into the woods, combing the area with several friends. They called my brother's name, and drove around in every direction as the sky grew dark and a heavy rain began to fall. After two hours of panicked and fruitless searching, my dad called the police. The missing-person report was filed at the Hillsborough County Sheriff's Department:

Subject's Name: Kushner, Jonathan Mark.
Date and Time Subject Left Home: 28 Oct 73, 12:30.
Location Last Seen: 7-11.
School Attendance: IDS.
Grade: 5th.
Height: 4 foot, 8 inches.
Weight: 85 Pounds.
Build: Slender.
Money Carried: $2.00.
Personal Habits: Nature Lover.

The police came to the house and made the following notes about my dad's account of what had happened: "Kushner did not witness victim leaving home. His 4 yrs old son David did. He told w/m Kushner that the victim said that if it rained he would call home for a way back. It rained, but the victim never called."

By the time Andy biked home later that afternoon, cops were parked all outside the house. They proceeded to the 7-Eleven to interview the clerk, a young woman named Ms. Perkins. She recalled seeing Jon in the store earlier. He was "outstanding," she said, "due to his pretty hair and appearance." She even remembered what he had bought: "about 30 cents' worth of plastic alligator bubblegum type candy," the report read. ". . . it was noted to be a plastic alligator snapping head and inside was filled with round tiny pieces of bubblegum."

By seven o'clock, the 7-Eleven had been transformed into a command post. The clerk told the police that there were several other kids there too. A brush fire had broken out next to a motorcycle shop across the street, and the kids had run off to see it. She told them kids always came through the woods: kids on bikes, kids barefoot, teenage girls, a girl in braces on horseback who wore a halter top and "bikini jeans."

The police investigators began calling on Jon's friends to see if they knew anything. The phone rang at the home of Paul Siddall. Jon's friend from school. "Have you seen Jonathan?" the policeman asked. Word was spreading around the neighborhood, and now it was reaching the kids. Paul's father took him in the car, and they roamed the vacant lots with a flashlight looking for his friend. Jon's friend Doug Chisholm recalled, "I cried my heart out and had a feeling that if he didn't come home, he was gone."

As night fell, the cops searched IDS and the surrounding area. They looked on the roof of a nearby elementary school and trailed up and down the path from the 7-Eleven to our house. An officer said it took him six minutes to walk down the four-hundred-yard path. They also searched Jon's room for clues. A cop found a watch on Jon's dresser, and a wallet containing two dollar bills and thirty-seven cents in change. They looked through his school papers to see if perhaps a bad grade had sent him running way, but found nothing to suggest this.

The search continued, even with my brother Andy taking part. "I was scared to death of finding something," he later told me, "but also it was a sense of purpose." Andy looked around to see people from all walks of life: farmers, professors, hippies, cops, neighbors, kids. "I had no idea that humanity comes together like that," he recalled. "This sense of community in Tampa—it blew my mind."

Jerry Smith, a colleague of my father's at USF, told me he could remember "spending a better part of the night beating the bushes and seeing if we can find something. It was late at night in the saw grass, and we had no idea what sort of beasts lived in all that stuff. But we were trying to do something useful."

At around seven thirty, the searchers found Jon's bike about twenty-five yards off the dirt path behind the store. It "appeared to have been deliberately hidden from view," the cops reported, and they took it for processing. The discovery of the bike was one of the few things I remembered from that week, how I had headed into Andy's room to tell him what I thought was good news: in my four-year-old brain, I thought they had found Jon. My recollection was that Andy was disappointed to learn that they had, in fact, found only his bike, but now, when I brought this up, he told me that wasn't the case. "I knew you were wrong," he said compassionately. "I knew they hadn't found him."

That night at our house, a reporter spoke with my father, who sat in a chair, smoking a cigarette. "The fact the bike was left there is frightening," my father said. Then the room fell quiet for a bit. "We're grateful to all that came out," my father added. "If we're trying to find anything good to feel about, that's it."

37

DONNA WITT had worked the late shift on October 27 and came home to sleep at eight the next morning. Before she went to bed, Tillman and Witt told her they were going hunting near the highway, and wanted to use her car. "Go ahead," she said, and went to bed.

Donna was woken up at about five that evening by her boy, Troy, who was holding a long piece of saltwater taffy. "Do you want candy?" he asked. The seven-year-old showed her some other candy his father had brought home for him that afternoon, Snappy Gator Gum. Troy had two of the toys—one red, one blue—and he was snapping the alligators' mouths shut as he squeezed their necks. Donna thought it was strange that Witt would buy her boy candy, since they rarely had extra money for such treats. "It's not like him to say he spent his last penny to bring candy home," she said later. But when Witt told her he had bought the candy, she didn't question it.

Donna came out of her room to find Tillman and Witt back from their day of hunting and watching TV. They said they were starving and asked her to fix them something to eat. Tillman seemed moody and quiet, and Witt was particularly irritable. He got even more wound up as Troy paraded around the room with his candy, offering it up. "Daddy," Troy said, "do you want some?"

"I bought it for you," Witt replied. "Used all my money to buy it. You eat it."

But the boy persisted, only making his stepfather more angry. "I don't want it," Witt said.

"John finally got irritated at him for pestering him," recalled Donna, who appeased her son by eating some of the candy herself.

The anxiety was already starting to wear at Witt from what he had done. "I tried to block out what happened by keeping busy," he told the police later. As Tillman sat inside watching TV, Witt told Donna it was time to go out and wash the car. This struck Donna as unusual, since ordinarily he'd take it to a car wash. He said he'd give her a hand, and the two went outside. Donna could see storm clouds gathering overhead. "There's not much use in washing the car because it's going to rain," she told him. "Why do it now?" But Witt insisted, and they washed the car until the sun went down and even as the rain began to fall.

At around ten fifteen that night, Donna was about to drive to work when she noticed that the car's gas tank was nearly empty. Angry, she jumped out and stormed back into the trailer, demanding to know why her husband hadn't filled the tank after his hunting trip. Witt snapped back and told her they hadn't gone out to the highway in Tampa after all. They had driven out toward Saint Petersburg but were low on gas, so they ended up at an orange grove. But he swore there wasn't even a half tank of gas when he left, something she refused to believe. "I know there was because I put it in there," she barked back as he poured himself a drink.

Donna drove to work in the pouring rain and called home from the hospital to let Witt know she'd arrived safely.

"I figured you did," he said.

"Are you drunk?" she asked.

"I'm getting that way."

"He was pretty well high," she recalled later. "He was giggling, something he very seldom ever does." Concerned that he was drinking more than usual, Donna told him to call her back later to let her know how drunk he was getting. "You wouldn't want me to embarrass you," he told her.

Donna arrived back home the next morning to take her boy to school, but Tillman and Witt had gone to work. She began cleaning the house and then noticed something unusual as she was dusting: a patch sitting on the bookcase of *Reader's Digest* magazines. It was green and white, and had a little blue owl on it. She figured it was some Boy Scouts patch of Tillman's.

Troy was busy playing with his new toys. "He was sitting on the floor, clicking alligators," she recalled later. "Drove me up a tree."

38

On the morning of October 29, people around the city opened their newspapers to read of my missing brother. Among them were Stan and Madelyn Rosenberg, former neighbors of ours from where we first lived in Tampa. My mother had brought them a pot roast shortly after they had moved in, and our families carpooled together to the synagogue. When Madelyn saw the headline in the paper, however, her mind couldn't grasp it. *Jonathan?* she thought. *Jonathan Kushner?*

"I get chills when I say it," she told me over coffee at the Village Inn restaurant near their home. Madelyn had long, dark hair, and Stan, a tanned retiree in a baseball cap, sat solemnly next to her. "How do you even comprehend that headline when you know the child?" She told me, "It was a name we knew. It was just an immediate connection: 'What can we do?' No one said, 'Oh, you need to help.' It was a feeling that this was something you had to do. Your psyche said, 'You need to be involved.' No one can go through this alone."

Stan called my father, who told him there was going to be a meeting that night at the local elementary school for volunteers to help in the search. Stan worked in real estate at the time, but he had been interested in police work since having grown up on cop TV shows in Cleveland. After college, he had taken an exam to become an officer and scored among the top test takers, getting an offer to join the force in Arkansas. But Madelyn wasn't about to move to the Deep South, so he acquiesced and moved to Tampa to work in real estate.

When he showed up at the school that evening, there was a crowd of volunteers, including friends and my father's students, each of whom was assigned a block of the area to search. Attorney Arnie Levine acted as the liaison with the investigators, and Mitch Silverman, who worked in the Criminal Justice Department at USF, lent his expertise. The cops had been searching all day, using aerial photographs from local builders. They had sent out land rovers, riders on horseback, and seven members of the Florida water rescue team to search every pond and drainage ditch in the area. With Jon having disappeared in the woods, Stan knew they needed people who could traverse the rough ground in the area, and he had an idea just where to find them: a biker bar. "You can go anywhere on a bike," Stan told me.

This wasn't just any biker bar, it was a rural hangout for the Outlaw Gang, the surliest bunch in town, and they didn't take kindly to outsiders. "If you weren't a biker, you didn't go in there," Stan recalled. But he didn't care. He parked his car—the only car in the lot—in front of the bar and went inside under watchful eyes. He showed the bartender a picture of my brother, and explained that he was missing and the family needed volunteers to search the woods. The bartender eyed him, then reached for a baseball bat—which he slammed down on the counter to get everyone's attention. "He had 'em shut up," Stan said, "and they listened to me. I had a picture of your brother and said, 'It all started in the field. He might be in the field somewhere.' "

The bikers trailed out of the lot behind Stan, who was now the unlikely commander of this unlikely search party. "I'm conducting something, and I didn't know what I was talking about," Stan recalled. As the days wore on, he solicited off-road vehicles from a local car dealer, including the biggest in town, Bill Currie Ford.

While people searched, Madelyn and other women tended to the house, preparing food, comforting one another, supporting my family. "I was in an altered state," my mother recalled. "People came in and took over—my parents, friends—everything was being taken care of. I was just hoisted in another dimension." At one point, when there was nothing to do, a woman came up to Madelyn and some others and said, "Okay, ladies, we gotta clean this fridge." As Madelyn recalled, "It was the only thing to do."

As the news spread, more and more people began coming to our house to help. Two women showed up from a faraway farm bearing casseroles. "You don't know us," one said. "We just thought you'd need some help." Our house teemed with disparate people from around town: professors, cops, bikers. Stan recalled Heinrich coming up to him and mentioning that "he'd never been around people who are Jewish."

Stan, a working-class guy, could relate, because he'd never been around so many academics. "It gave me a feeling for these guys," he recalled. "How would I know about professors except from going to school?"

Madelyn went on, "So many different groups came together in this one common purpose," she said of the search for my brother, "to find him."

"It was just an outstanding outpouring," recalled Espy Ball, the psychologist who had worked with Jon on his difficulties in school. "I have never been so impressed by a group of people supporting two of their dear ones in my life. I was floored by what I saw—your parents earned part of that, and part of that was just a huge number of people out there that have that sense of community and are ready to help, whatever happens." Arnie Levine told me, "The community came forward in a situation that I'd never experienced before or since."

At one point, a man in the house grew distressed, unable to grasp the possibility that Jon had been attacked by strangers. He began speaking loudly about how that just wasn't possible, that this had to be the act of someone who knew Jon, who knew my family, that there had to be a reason for what had happened. Rumors had spread that perhaps my father, who had been recently outspoken in support of Israel, could have made us a target for retaliation. Even my mother worried about this being some form of vengeance, as her mind struggled for a reason. "Your father could be really tough," she recalled, "and I know some students probably didn't like him at all. My thought was maybe someone at the university did this to get back at Dad, and that made me mad at Dad."

As Ball heard the man talking, he felt increasingly uncomfortable, afraid that my parents would overhear this and feel even worse. "If you're in a situation where you don't know where your son is, you don't want to be hearing this," he recalled. But he knew that this was all just the result of frustration boiling over; of everyone's individual struggle to impose order on something that was beyond comprehension. "Everybody there was working out, in some form, their own sense of horror and fright," Ball said.

Of course, my family was working through these emotions too. "It was a fucking nightmare," Andy recalled. "It was hell, the weight of it was horrendous, I said I thought he was dead for sure, and believed after the first night that it was over. It was horrible." He went on: "The week he was missing was sheer torture and incredibly traumatizing."

"I remember looking at myself in the mirror," my mother said, "and thinking, *How come I look the way I am, but I'm so not me?*" They had shut the door to Jon's room and closed it off while they waited. "I remember how awful it was," my mother said, "closing off the room during that time, shutting the door."

The fear was spreading to concern about the safety of Andy and me. With Jon missing, my parents worried about what, if anything, might happen to us. "It was scary to be in the house," my mother told me. "We were so afraid for you kids." They had workers set up spotlights outside the house for extra safety and kept them on throughout the night—just in case Jon, or someone else, came back. "During the search, you couldn't be out of our sight," my mother recalled. "We felt you could be targeted."

My father, at the same time, did his best to keep my mother insulated. "He was talking to people; he was very involved," my mom said. "He was trying to protect me and say, 'It's okay, let me take care of this.' He was wanting me to be sheltered." But my mother had always been involved in everything—her work, her causes—and this was no different. "I said 'No,'" she recalled. "'I want to be totally involved.'"

While the visitors to our house provided tremendous support, they couldn't help but sneak glances at my family, to look for clues as to how we were doing, how we could possibly survive such impossible stress. "People were saying, 'I wouldn't be able to handle this like that,'" Ball observed.

My family handled it in a few ways. When the emotions became too great, we would leave the crowd and go into our rooms and cry. My father's headaches were still coming, and he would lie in bed and put on his oxygen mask until the pain went away. But they would return to the crowd, to the friends, to the strangers, and they would connect with them and their experience of this madness, hugging them, thanking them, comforting them. They were all discovering the incredible human capacity for support and love, and this, in part, was what enabled them to survive.

"Both of them would come out and in effect take care of the community because they could really see that each of those couples and each of those individuals was going through their own [experience]," Ball recalled. "I just remember the picture of your mother moving so gracefully among people, touching them, hugging them. She had this manner of simply putting them at ease, not only themselves but giving them the chance to see that she was coping with this."

Jim Bradley, the principal of IDS at the time, recalled seeing my mother comforting a woman who was breaking down in our house. "She was doing the soothing and the strengthening," he said to me. "Your family was a pillar of strength."

As I heard these stories, I began to realize what precisely enabled, among other things, my parents to survive: the unexpected reserves that both had within themselves and the unexpected reserves that came from our community. “In the face of this kind of event, a serious loss,” Ball said, “I will promise you, you can’t even imagine the resources that you have. There is a strength that is in there that you can’t even imagine.”

39

Students from USF, which had partly shut down to help with the search, made the rounds with fliers. It had a picture of Jon from the yearbook. It read "$5,000 reward for information leading to the recovery of Jonathan Kushner," along with a description of what he was last seen wearing, based on my recollection at the time. "Help us find this boy," the flier concluded. It soon papered the town: the Speede Shop, the In and Out Food Store, Kash n' Karry, McDonald's, and so on.

"This has been the greatest response we have ever seen," Sheriff Malcolm Beard told the local paper, "and we covered territory in a few days that would have taken the department several weeks."

The media was constantly at our doorstep, the press coverage just another extension of the search. "I welcomed all of that," my mother recalled. "I felt they're here to help us." The support extended beyond the house to the school Jon was attending at the time. On Monday morning, the FBI was on campus, pulling teachers and students out of class to speak with them as helicopters circled overhead. A nationwide broadcast went out to all police agencies.

As the hours unfolded, the cops began going around the neighborhood to talk with the kids. One ten-year-old told the cops he'd seen my brother the day before his disappearance, playing in an abandoned house wearing a football jersey. Another said he saw him playing in a creek near a dead-end road. Another said he'd seen him coming out of a Christmas shop, but, clearly, because we were Jewish, was confused.

As they spoke to the kids, a picture of Jon's behavior emerged. One kid described Jon as "a quiet and shy boy, and is not the type to initiate a conversation. However, he will speak when spoken to. He is very organized and neat in his habits. He will occasionally throw a temper tantrum with cause but is not of a mind to run away from home." Jon was on the soccer team. Jon was very agile. He had a loud voice when he played sports but was otherwise quiet. One girl told the police she heard the whole thing was "a joke" and that Jon was staying with friends.

Fear and guilt began infecting people there. Sandra Parks, the teacher who was also the mother of one of Jon's friends, struggled to make sense of what had happened. Jon, she told me, was a "trusting soul," and she wondered if he would have gone off with strangers willfully. She also realized in horror that, just a day before Jon had gone missing, she had been at school, and had a group of students who asked if they could go to the 7-Eleven during a break, something that was not uncommon.

"We put emphasis on creating independent learners," she recalled. "It was our practice, during off-hours, to let kids from IDS follow the path to convenience stores to get ices." But that day, she had said no, because there wasn't time. And she reeled in horror to think that perhaps those kids would have suffered the same fate too.

"Children wanted to help," recalled Principal Bradley. Though he and the others were convinced that Jon would not be found on campus, they decided to empower the students by letting them search the area. "It was just some way to make them feel a little less impotent about the whole thing," he said.

As I learned later, however, the kids were going through traumas that were similar to mine, as they tried to grasp this bizarre and frightening reality. There had been a monster movie, *The Legend of Boggy Creek*, the year before, and John Wing, my brother's friend, felt an eerie connection to what was happening around him. He thought about a scene in which a boy gets chased out of the woods as the beast screams behind him. "To us, that was indicative of the whole situation that we were witnessing," Wing recalled, "You had this sinister woods off in the distance, where one of us had been gobbled up by who knows what. It was kind of like Hollywood fiction come to life for us."

There were other fears around campus too: that one of their own might be responsible. The cops suspected that a particular teacher might have been involved in the crime. The teacher was rumored to have spent time with kids after school. He would take them for sleepovers and show them his model train set in his house. The cops went to Jon's friends Chisholm and Siddall for information. Siddall said the teacher had spent the night at his house, taking care of him while his parents were away. The cops asked if the teacher had made any "homosexual advances" toward him, but Siddall said no. Chisholm, who had been at the teacher's house to go swimming after school, said the teacher hadn't come on to him either.

After word spread about a teenage boy who had been spotted

reading a book on witchcraft, he was interviewed by the cops. The boy told them he was studying the subject and had heard that there was a group of Satan worshippers north of Tampa, which, he surmised, might be capable of kidnapping someone for a human sacrifice.

No matter how outlandish the stories, the police had to explore every possible lead. My father had to answer the phone at the house every time it rang. There were prank calls, people claiming to have or even be Jon. One person called the cops and said, "If you want to find the Kushner boy, check the first house east of Dale Mabry on the Van Dyke Road." Then he hung up. The lead went nowhere.

The local police hadn't experienced anything like this either. "This was the first time to see something of this magnitude," recalled James Walker, then a twenty-six-year-old officer who had been working on school safety programs when he heard the news. "Heinrich pulled in everyone to work on that case," Walker told me. The case was unique because Jon's bike had been discovered so early on, which immediately suggested foul play. "It was a big mystery," Walker said. Instead of having the normal one or two detectives on a missing-person case, there were dozens.

Sheriff's Major Heinrich was, as Walker recalled, "very intense as far as his determination to solve this. He was pulling people off their normal duties, calling the air force to dispatch heat-seeking planes. I'd never seen these kinds of resources before." Walker took on the job of coordinating volunteers at the University of South Florida, where my dad worked. Every morning, forty or fifty officers, FBI agents, and others gathered in a classroom there to get briefed on the latest leads and coordinate their plan. Volunteers began lining up at the university; each one was registered and given an area to go door-to-door around town canvasing for leads.

Walker felt odd being there among the same students whom he had restrained during an earlier demonstration against the Vietnam War. "I was out there throwing tear gas at them across campus," he recalled. "It was kinda alien, you felt outta place, but the spirit of cooperation there was on both sides."

As the investigation continued, it spread among the children, spreading the story, spreading the fear like a virus. Something was changing. The world they'd taken for granted was coming into a dark new light. Assemblies were held at local schools, as a deputy explained the story and asked for any information on Jon or stories about kids' adventures on the path where he'd disappeared.

A girl said she'd been on a horse in the woods when she saw a white man lingering by a car with rusted headlights. A boy said he had been walking when he saw two men who were hunting in the area and told him to go away. Another girl said she was walking along a wall near the store when a man grabbed her by the ankle and started laughing before letting her go.

On November 2 the police interviewed a girl who didn't know Jon but said that, a couple of weeks earlier, she had been walking along the trail to the 7-Eleven with a friend, when, as the cops reported, "she observed a w/m in the wooded area, standing beside a yellow vehicle, and holding a bow and arrow. States the subject pointed the bow at them and told them to leave the area, which they did. States she cannot describe the subject. No further information."

40

On Saturday, November 4, seven days after my brother went missing, Donna Witt was working the late shift again at Tampa General Hospital, when she saw a sign taped up on a wall. It was a flier announcing that a group of volunteers was going to help search for Jonathan Kushner that afternoon, and anyone else who wanted to assist could come along. Donna, like most others in Tampa, had been following the saga all week. One day she had been sitting in her trailer with her husband when the story came on the TV news. "That's awful," Witt had said, and then told Troy to get up and change the channel.

Donna wanted to join the search party, but after working all night, she wasn't up to it, and she drove home to her husband. When she got back, Witt had just returned from camping overnight with Tillman. But he hadn't just gone camping the night before at all. He was up at Withlacoochee forest with Tillman, burying the jar with Jon's penis and scrotum, which he had been hiding at the house in a small bottle, by a fence post. Donna made herself comfortable and told Witt about the sign she'd seen in the hospital. "If I hadn't worked all night," she said, "I think I would have gone today."

"You don't want to," Witt said. "There's too many snakes and things." It was just the thing to dissuade her. "I'm frightened to death of snakes," she told the police later.

But the pressure had been wearing on Witt all week. "Depression hit me, and I couldn't stand the emotions that were on my mind and stomic [*sic*]," he wrote later in his statement to the police. He kept having his stepson change the TV channel whenever the news of my brother came on, and tried not to listen at work as people discussed the missing boy. At one point, he admitted later, "I wanted to give myself up but did not because the boy's body had been cut." But by now, the stress had proven too much. "After a week of pure hell, I desided [*sic*] that I would tell my wife, knowing she would turn me in," he wrote later in his statement. "And to make sure she did, I tell her everything."

The next night, Witt had Donna make him several highballs, and the drunker he got, the more sullen he became. Finally, he stumbled into the kitchen while she was washing dishes, and said something about hating people. Then he asked her a question: "Would you hate me if I had done anything?"

"No," she said.

"Then he sit down at the table," Donna recalled later, "and he looked funny, you know . . . like something was bothering him, and he couldn't know whether to tell me or not to tell me." She tried to reassure him. "Just tell me anything you want to," she said. "You know I'm always with you, stay with you."

Finally, Witt spoke. "Do you know where the candy come from?" he said, referring to the Snappy Gator Gum and taffy.

"Why, no. Why don't you tell me?"

Then he hesitated. "The candy I brought Troy that night."

"Yes."

"Do you know where I got it?"

"Just what you said."

"Well, it come from somebody. You know that little boy that's missing?"

"Yeah."

"You know how it feels to sit at work and hear the guys talking about 'I wonder where he's at' or 'What's happened to him?'" He paused. "I'm the one that done it." He went on. "You hate me, don't you?"

"No, you can tell me anything you want to. What did you do to him?"

Witt told her he'd shot him with a bow and arrow, an odd lie that admitted his killing but not in the manner in which it had actually happened. "You're going to turn me in, aren't you?"

"No," Donna said, as she tried to keep him talking. "Well, where's he at?"

"He's in a safe place nobody can find him."

"Where?"

Witt said he was camouflaged and buried out in the woods. As Donna persisted in questioning him, Witt spun his story more, telling her he'd shot the boy in the stomach and then cut the arrow free. And that Tillman was with him. "We buried him," Witt said.

"Well, how?"

"You see that knife laying in there?"

Donna recognized the blade. It was Tillman's old hunting knife that they used to slice bacon. "Yeah."

Witt picked up the knife and showed it to her. It seemed different now, she thought—brightly metallic, as if it had just been cleaned. Witt told her they had used it to cut the arrow from the boy's stomach and that Tillman had then used it to dig the grave. All the digging had made it dull now, even though they'd polished it up, he told her, handing her the blade. "See how shiny it is," he said. "But it won't cut a thing now."

"I took it and ran it up my arm," Donna told the police later, "and it wouldn't cut the hairs, and used to, it would. It wouldn't do anything." Donna began to grow increasingly anxious, pressing him for information on where they buried the body, and fearful that there was evidence in her car that they had used. "That means you had to put him in the trunk," she said. "Wouldn't there be a lot of blood?"

"I think there's a couple of spots of blood in the rubber raft that's in the car," he said. The more they talked, the more nervous Witt became. He told her how he had felt the night before when she had talked about joining the search for the boy. "Can you imagine how I felt," he said, "you setting there on the floor talking about going on the hunt for him, my own wife?"

Witt grew anxious about being caught. "If any chance they ever find out that I did it," he told her, "if they ask you anything, I never told you nothing. You know what they'd do to you. You'd be in trouble too." He said he was worried about Tillman turning them in, and suggested he might do something drastic to Tillman if necessary to keep him quiet. Witt sat back in his chair and laughed disturbingly as he enlisted Donna in a plan to see how resolved Tillman was to stay silent. "When Gary comes home, do you want to shake him up a little?" he said.

Donna was nervous now, and humored him. "Sure," she said.

"Well, we have to think of something to ask him to let him know that you know without panicking."

"What do you want me to do?" she asked. "You want me to ask him about the candy?" She couldn't believe that Witt was telling her the truth. It was too outrageous. Her mind immediately went to the alligator candy that she had eaten the week before. The thought that it had come from the murdered boy sickened her. "That's when I asked about the candy," she told the cops later, "because that was all that stuck in my mind because I ate some of the candy. You know. It's hard to take."

But Witt had other plans. "No, don't ask about that," he said, and then picked up the knife. "Tell him how much this knife cost. Tell him the next time to use a shovel."

A bit later, Tillman returned, and Donna played along. She walked over to the TV and picked up the knife, letting out a nervous laugh. "By the way, this cost me thirteen dollars," she said to Tillman out of the blue, "Next time, use a shovel."

Tillman looked surprised as he glanced over at Witt, wondering what was going on. As Donna headed down the hall to the bathroom, she could hear Witt continue to play along. He was trying to cover up the fact that he had confessed and instead make it look like Donna was on to them. "The FBI and everything else is out looking for him," he told Tillman. "But who finds out? My wife."

When Donna came back from the bathroom, Witt and Tillman were sitting quietly. Unsure of what to do, Donna sat beside them in silence. When she glanced up, they were eyeing her. Unable to take it anymore, she pushed herself up and muttered an excuse, the first thing that popped into her mind. "I have to have some candy," she said, and walked off to make fudge in the kitchen. "I was just mixed up," she told the cops later.

As Donna lay in bed watching TV later in the night, Witt came in and punched her lightly in the shoulder. "What's the matter?" he said.

"Nothing," she replied. "I'm just watching TV, and I'm tired, you know." He climbed into bed beside her.

"Well," she said, "what did Gary say about me knowing?"

Witt told her that Tillman got the message—that Donna could be trusted. But what about Tillman turning them in, Donna wondered. "You don't think he'll tell on you?" she asked.

"Let's forget about it," he said. "It's old business." Then he rolled over and went to sleep, as Donna lay awake the rest of the night, pondering what to do. The next morning, she fixed Witt breakfast as usual and told him she had errands to run: take Troy to school and then stop at the bank. "I'll be gone for quite a while this morning," she said.

Witt didn't make anything of it and went off to work. As soon as he left, Donna left her boy in the kitchen with breakfast and went outside. Popping open her trunk, she took out the raft and dragged it into her bedroom, shutting the door behind her. Donna began looking for spots of blood, taking a wash rag and rubbing off a few stains to see if they were red. Then she went into Tillman's things and began searching for the patch. Troy came up behind her. "What are you looking in there for?" he asked.

41

BY NOVEMBER 5, now eight days after Jon vanished, we were losing hope. The organized search of the area, after extending so far from where Jon could have been, was called off. The investigation continued, but we were on the verge of becoming another statistic, another family who would have to bear the unbearable possibility of having no resolution at all—a fate perhaps even more difficult than finding that a child had been killed. Without answers, one can imagine anything, and that is a hell all its own.

At one point, my parents agreed to let the psychic come to the house, despite their skepticism. "I said 'Fine,' and I talked to her," my mother recalled, "and it was like anybody come in. 'You got a Seeing Eye dog, bring him in!' Anything." The psychic said she thought Jon had been taken by four men as vengeance for some kind of drug deal. When she said she sensed hope, my brother greeted the news not just with skepticism but also fury. "I was feeling hopeless and angry," he recalled.

In Jon's room, my father drew the blinds shut, something we rarely did during the day. My mother, still trying to cling to hope, reacted with dismay. "When your dad would do that, I would never want him to do that," she recalled. "I would want him to open blinds and not be a house of mourning." But we were running out of light. On the evening of November 4, my father went on the local news to plead for information. Maybe someone would finally step forward.

The next morning, Deputy Walker was at the Hillsborough Sheriff's Department when a woman called saying she had information on the Kushner boy. After a week of fruitless leads, he wasn't optimistic. But when he saw the expression on the cop who was fielding the call, he knew this one was different. "I remember sitting and seeing the intensity on his face," Walker recalled. "I knew it was important."

The woman said that her husband had made a drunken confession about killing the missing boy, and that there was evidence in her trailer: candy and a Camp Keystone patch. To aid the investigation, the police had refrained from releasing certain details about the case—such as what Jon had bought at the 7-Eleven and the patch on his shorts. This way, if a caller mentioned these items, they would know the call was legit.

"I just got to find out two things," the woman went on. "About the candy, because he had emphasized that's where the candy came from. The type. I knew what type I ate, and that's why I called. I wanted to know about it. And I wanted to know about the patch because he said it belonged to the little boy." The more she spoke, however, the more nervous she seemed to become. The cops, who couldn't trace the call, feared she might panic and hang up, and they struggled to ascertain her location.

"Where you at?" the cop on the phone asked.

She told him an intersection in West Tampa, and the cops sped on their way. When they arrived, however, she was gone—along with their first, and only, tangible lead all week. They feared the worst as they searched the area to no avail, and began driving away. But as they went down the road, they noticed a car broken down on the side of the street. When they pulled over to help the person, they realized it was their caller. Her name was Donna Witt. "Just to show you how the Lord works," the cop later recalled "she tried to leave, but she had a flat tire. Had she been gone, we might not have ever solved that one."

That afternoon, Sheriff's Major Heinrich told Stan Rosenberg he had a run to make, and asked if he'd like to tag along. "Sure," Stan replied, always eager to learn more about policing. "I'm enjoying riding with you." The two had become unlikely friends over the week, and Heinrich showed his appreciation by letting Stan call him by his first name. At one point, Heinrich had walked up to Stan and squeezed his arm. "Ah, you'll do fine," he said and then walked away. "I didn't know what he was talking about," Stan recalled. But he found out in the weeks to come. After our case, Heinrich offered Stan the opportunity he'd long wanted: to become a cop and come work for him. With his wife's blessing, Stan accepted. As they rode off in Heinrich's police car on November 5, Stan asked about the destination. "Where we going?"

"Well," Heinrich replied, "I think we got one of the guys."

They arrived at the Shady Grove Mobile Home Park in Thonotosassa, and walked inside a beige trailer with brown trim and a TV antenna on top. Tearfully, Donna Witt told them everything she knew, and the police knew they had found their men. They seized evidence: two stains scraped from the trunk of the Plymouth, one stain cut from the trunk mat; one rusted bowie knife; one long drill bit; forty-six arrows, four bows, one crossbow; a book, *Engineering Drawing and Design*, with the Camp Keystone patch between pages eight and nine; a two-man yellow and blue raft; and two Snappy Gators, one red, one blue.

At two thirty, police cars pulled up to the Singleton Shrimp Company in Tampa, where they found Gary Tillman in the employees' locker room and arrested him. At three thirty, Heinrich, two other police officers—Lieutenant Arnie Myers and Roebuck—as well as members of the FBI, and Rosenberg pulled up to the Burger Chef fast-food restaurant, where they had been told Witt was working. Roebuck climbed a ladder in the back and spotted the suspect working on an air-conditioning unit on the roof. Witt, seeing the officer with a gun at his side, stood quickly and raised his pipe wrench over his head.

Roebuck told him to drop the tool, but Witt still held it, looking around nervously. Again Roebuck told him to drop it, but to no avail. Heinrich, who had climbed up to the roof as well, then ordered Witt to drop the wrench or he could get hurt. Finally, Witt complied, and as soon as they got him down the ladder, he was cuffed and advised of his constitutional rights. "That was the first time in my career that I wanted to pull my gun and kill somebody," Heinrich told Stan later.

When Walker heard of the arrests, he knew that all their hard work, all the media attention, and the actions of the community had helped to wear down Witt and, ultimately, his wife. What seemed like "an impossible" task, as he put it, was not insurmountable after all. "His wife saw that it wasn't going to go away," Walker recalled. "We were going to keep the intensity, and no matter how insignificant the lead was . . . that had a lot to with her coming forward."

After Tillman led the cops to the crime scene, the case against him and Witt moved quickly. Now in custody, Witt asked the lieutenant to tell his wife he loved her, then he sat down to write his confession. He ran out of paper and asked for more so that he could continue. He asked how to spell *definite*, and *decision*, and *bicycle*. Finally, he set down his pen and began to cry. "Why didn't the boy wait ten minutes?" he said. "I was getting ready to go home."

The cops asked Witt if he and Tillman had planned to kill someone that day. Witt said they had planned to do this, but, as the police report explained, "not anyone in particular, as they were just hunting and that when rabbit hunting, you don't pick a certain rabbit to kill, but rather take what comes along." Later he asked to talk with the jail chaplain, who came in and offered to share a prayer. "I don't believe I'm worthy of a prayer because of what we did," Witt said.

"Let the Lord be your judge," the chaplain replied.

Tillman, for his part, put the blame on Witt. "I do what John tells me," he told the police, "because he is a friend; he will not tell me to do anything that is wrong."

Witt and Tillman were soon taken to the Hillsborough courthouse for their hearing. Heinrich dispatched a decoy car there, to divert the throng of reporters and onlookers who had gathered for the hearing. But with the case having received so much attention, a crowd of sixty people gathered outside to leer and jeer. Heinrich led Witt, who was dressed in his white short-sleeve air-conditioning-company shirt, from the car. Witt shuffled inside in his shackles, sullen and pallid. Tillman, dressed in a long-sleeve Yamaha motorcycle shirt, was led in behind him, as the police warded off the crowd.

"Hanging is too good!" shouted one man.

"Dirty creep!" a woman yelled. "They ought to shoot ya!"

Inside, after a five-hour hearing in which the two pled not guilty, a Hillsborough grand jury indicted Witt and Tillman for the murder of my brother. The court clerk burst into tears while she was reading the indictment and had to have the circuit judge continue for her. An FBI agent was seen later at a church pew, pale and forlorn, his eyes welling. "You just won't believe it when you hear the whole story," he told a reporter. "It's incredible."

Witt and Tillman were tried separately. After being interviewed by psychiatrists, Witt was found to have a "long-standing personality disorder" including "extreme sexual perversion," but was not deemed insane. Psychiatrists found, however, that he had, according to court documents, "an incurable propensity to commit future violent crimes," and that he was a "menace to society" and "a sexual pervert."

During Witt's trial in February 1974, his attorney tried to pin the murder on Tillman, who had struck and gagged my brother. "My client is guilty of sexual perversion," he conceded. "It's shocking. It's gruesome. It's filthy. It's abominable. I shudder at the thought when I think of my three boys. I'm not asking you to forget it. I'm asking you to remember when the boy died and to try and show intent in relation to these events. It has nothing to do with if Johnny Paul Witt intended to kill this boy . . . you don't get electrocuted for sexual perversion, and you can't kidnap a dead person."

But the assistant state attorney who handled the prosecution wasn't having any of it. "He [Witt] knew that whoever was coming down that path was a dead man," he said. "He knew that from the beginning. I will submit it was a partnership with one common plan: to kill Jonathan Kushner. Afterward there was a constant intent to conceal a crime, a very good plan, and not a man who was panicked."

A twelve-member jury deliberated for two and a half hours before coming back with a verdict for Witt: guilty of first-degree murder. When a psychiatrist who had interviewed Witt was asked if Witt had shown remorse after the crime, he replied: "He said the only mistake they made was getting a kid whose old man was famous." Sitting in the courtroom was Donna Witt. Though she had been the one to turn in her husband, something that our family appreciated deeply, there was never any contact between us. She sobbed as the verdict came in. The next day, Witt was sentenced to die in the electric chair.

Three months later, Tillman pled guilty for his role in the murder, enabling him to receive life in prison instead of the electric chair. In the weeks leading up to his trial, Tillman had been ingesting metal in his cell, perhaps to act more insane or even to commit suicide—it was unclear. At one point, on the way back to jail from court, Tillman told the deputies that, as they reported later, "numerous persons should be very concerned if he [Tillman] ever escaped, as he would seek revenge." The people on his list included members of law enforcement, as well as his parents and sister. "Tillman stated that he would start revenge at the bottom of the list so that the people on the top would worry more," the report concluded.

Given his schizophrenia, there had been much deliberation behind the scenes among the prosecutors and friends of our family about this. People feared that pursuing the death penalty for Tillman could result in an insanity plea, one that could, ultimately, see him being released from a mental institution and back on the streets at some point. "The decision to accept a sentence of life imprisonment rather than risk his early release from a mental institution has been reached with a deep sense of public responsibility for the safety and security of the people of this state," the Hillsborough County state attorney said.

Later, when the cops asked Tillman why he did it, he said, "I didn't have anything better to do." He said his intention the whole day was pleasing Witt. "The only thing I was interested in was keeping him happy," he said. When they asked him why he cut the patch from Jon's shorts, he said, "Nobody should ever throw away a patch like that; they are too hard to get."

Tillman's family was struggling to make sense of what he had done, and discussed approaching my family—something they never got the strength to do. "How do you go up and knock on a man's door and say, 'I'd like to talk to you for a moment and apologize for my son being one of the accused murderers of your son?' " Tillman's father, Lige, told a reporter. "I think that they know—I hope to God they do—how sorry we are about this. There's nothing in the world we wouldn't do to undo what has been done. There is no way to do it. I wish to God we could."

Long before the widespread fear over abductions spread around the country on cable and local news, Tampa, in the years following Jon's murder, was reeling. "That was a seminal event in that ability of kids to simply get on their bikes and go," recalled Dr. Ball. "All of us became more careful."

"You start telling your kids, 'Don't go down to the corner, don't go down the street,'" Madelyn Rosenberg recalled. "You have this thought in your head: you can only play in our yard, you can't go anywhere else."

IDS stopped letting kids go to the convenience store. It was a radical impact on the place that so exemplified and cultivated the freedom of the times. "It was such a safe and loving place," recalled Parks, "these people were themselves innocents. In the middle of all this innocence, lurking just a hundred yards from this cocoon we all lived in, was this perversity. I mean, that was the end of innocence and the belief that if you associated with like people, and you were loving and you were nurturing of one another, that somehow you weren't going to be touched by evil. And yet here was Jonathan, who was kind of the major symbol of that, living right at the edge of the campus itself, the most innocent among us. It was staggering."

The police department began a campaign to create safe houses for kids in trouble. They distributed blue stickers in the shape of hands that homeowners were to affix to their windows in case anyone was ever in trouble. But while Ball limited how far his own children could go after this tragedy, he already sensed that that fear was coming at a price. Despite the horror of what happened to our family, he knew, children were more likely to die from an accident inside the home than to get abducted and killed. "That's where danger is," he told me, "but that's not where danger is in the minds of the parents. It's sad for children because of that inability to get the proper distance from parents in order to feel 'I can stand on my own two feet.'" He feared that, with the rush to schedule after-school activities rather than let kids roam, kids would suffer "the loss of that independent play."

Sometime after this, Ball penned my parents a letter. "I hope you're doing well," he wrote, "and Lord knows I don't know day in and day out how you're coming with this, but I will tell you that for the rest of my life there will never be an October that I don't think of Jonathan."

42

For years, I had been tormented by what I didn't know; my imagination had run wild. I struggled to reconcile the snippets of information I picked up from kids at school, from newspaper accounts, from my family's occasional comments around the house. My brain had worked overtime, sometimes self-destructively, as it sought to provide the missing pieces, the empty pages, the scattered strips of film.

Jon's murderers had long not even been real to me. They were faces from which I turned away, bogeymen who lurked in the bushes outside the sliding glass door. Learning their stories, their backgrounds, their plans, was something that, as painful as it was at times, settled some of my fears and worries. I could put faces to them now, hear their conversations. Perhaps I had never really wanted to look at the faces of evil, to acknowledge that evil truly exists and lurks in places we least suspect. Perhaps I had never really wanted to feel this in all its terrible reality, to know that people can be so monstrous, that monsters are among us, and, yet, knowing this, to find a way to survive and live.

This was a question I returned to, at last, with my mother sometime after I had concluded most of my research. How did you survive? I asked. How did you live? This wasn't just a question on my mind. It had been posed by our rabbi, Sandy Hahn, during the memorial service for my brother shortly after his death, as he faced a crowd of over a thousand people at our synagogue. "We have gathered here to search for some meaning in what's happened," he said, "if that's possible."

For my mother, the search began at some point during the awful days that followed the news of Jon's death. On one hand, there was resolution that the murderers had been caught and that justice was going to take over. Though my parents had not been active supporters of the death penalty, there was a conviction that Witt's sentence was best for society. "I felt personally that this was like a nuclear threat," my mother told me. "This is the biggest thing that can happen to people, we must all be protected from this monster . . . to put him in jail, who knows how long he'd be there or what would happen in the future, it was the best protection for society just to get rid of him."

But despite Witt's death sentence and the fact that Tillman had gotten life, this didn't resolve the loss. For each of us, that time was a dark blur of individual suffering, each of us dealing with it in our way, just as everyone deals with death in a personal manner. My parents had to not only find some way to survive this themselves but also to support and nurture Andy and me through the chaos as well.

"You had something severed from you," my mother told me. "Jon and you, you just adored him, and he just adored you, and then it was just ripped from you. And there you were, four years old and all this tumult and craziness. How do you explain what happened to you? You were confused, you were scared. I remember siting in the living room when we found out what happened, and Andy was there, and you, and just protecting you and loving you."

We couldn't talk about Jon, couldn't even say the word *murder*—not even in the decades to follow. I had always wondered why we were so silent about Jon, but my mother explained the obvious answer: "It was too scary," she said.

"It was just too painful," Andy told me as well.

But there's a price for living in silence: the isolation that comes with grief. I had experienced this myself for so long, the consequence of silence, the pain of it. My family was a family of storytellers, repeating tales of our lives over and over again, refining them along the way. But this story of Jon was never told. Death leaves trails of mutes. People don't know what to say to others who are grieving. They fear upsetting them, they don't know how to behave. But as my family learned, people who are grieving are desperate for support, for connection. It's always better to reach out to someone and just say simply, "I'm sorry," to let them know you're thinking about them, to give them a hug, and feel assured that that alone is enough.

As I heard my mother tell me of her struggles, of their efforts to transform their personal pain into social action, I began to appreciate even more how the three *C*s—community, compassion, and connection—are, perhaps, the fundamental ways that people survive not only death but also any kind of struggle and horror in life. But with the death of a child, this gets even more challenging. And it was challenging for my parents despite their activities. "I remember guilt when I laughed; how do you laugh?" my mother recalled. "How do you get into life and enjoy it, and when you laugh you feel guilty about it?"

One day my mother handed me some old yellowed papers to help me understand firsthand how she endured this question, how she struggled for answers, for meaning, for hope. It was the journal she had kept over the first few years following Jon's death. I read them in one sitting, following her early months of suffering, her dreams of Jon, her desire to speak out, to hear his name. As I read, I realized that she had been on a journey similar to my own. She didn't want to lose Jon to the annals of the past. She wanted to preserve his story, get it down before it disappeared. "How good that we're doing this," she wrote in July 1975, "making a record of our memories of Jon, our feelings, all of this helping to save Jon, to hang on to him, not forget."

Many times, she had despaired over the taboo surrounding death in our culture, the fear that prevented even the most compassionate people from discussing memories and feelings. "Why are people so afraid that talking about, thinking about, looking at a picture of a dead person is morbid?" she wrote. "It's so wrong and painful to live that way. Let's celebrate Jon. Let's laugh about him. Let's remember him. He is still part of our lives. Why can't we learn a different way to deal with death?"

There had been times she wanted to scream his name out loud, from the top of the Skyride at Busch Gardens, from the back of the synagogue, to remember him, to celebrate him, and to exorcise the pain inside her. "You'd think the body, the head, would split apart during the most intense grieving," she wrote. "But then tears and tears, building up and bursting out over and over, spasms of grief, constant and exhausting." And yet she could feel the pain becoming a part of her, finding its indelible groove but never vanishing. "Time goes by," she wrote, "days spill on, routines, appointments, diversions, some fun, a trip, somebody sick, on and on, time goes and grief finds a niche, a place, and settles in and goes along, too, included in everything. 'I'm here,' says Grief. 'Never mind me, just go about your business.' "

Jon's murder was real, it was permanent, part of our family, part of our community, and we had the responsibility to survive. "We must live," she wrote on October 28, 1975, on the second anniversary of Jon's death, "We must live with this pain of no Jon, for each of us all, Andy, David, especially, for Gil and me, for my parents, for friends who need to have us show them we *can* live with horror." And more than anything, it was our shared survival of the murder that enabled us to live. "I think that is the only way to make it, really, when all is said and done," my mother wrote the following October, "to have love and support from humans who breathe love and hug comfort."

Toward the end of her journal, her entries became less frequent. Life resumed its pace. There were joys and sorrows, births and deaths. There would never be closure, but there was something else that came with the passing time, as I read on the last page of her journal, from August 1977, nearly four years after Jon died: a way of living with death that brought new meaning to life.

"I treasure what I treasure," she wrote. "I am aware of the temporariness of relationships and life itself. I am aware of what matters and turns me on. Did Jon give me this gift? I believe so. My sweet, sweet, sweetness. I thank you for that. I carry you with me forever unseen now, just as I did when you were snuggling in my uterus through the streets of Jerusalem, unseen but filling my belly and my mind, part of our family even before you were born . . . part of our family now after your life. Thank you for this capacity to love and understand. Do you still know that you are loved?"

43

For so long, I had felt a disconnect with Jon's death, perhaps because I was so young at the time. It was my family, but it wasn't my family. It felt so unreal, as though the story had happened to someone else. But reading my mother's words, after all my research and interviews, made me feel more connected than ever before. This wasn't just some mother who had lost a son, this was my mom. And it wasn't just the thoughts and feelings of the mother of a murdered child, it was a document on the taboos that still exist around death and dying, the aloneness that people endure, and how, in the end, it is other people who can help us survive.

Each of us had always pursued our dreams—my mother in childbirth education, my father in anthropology, my brother in music, me in writing—against whatever obstacles we faced. For Andy and me in particular, since we started our careers after Jon's death, life felt urgent, and there was never time to wait or sacrifice what we wanted to achieve most. "We all came out of this more determined to not let it crush us," Andy reflected. "It's like what they said after 9/11: we can't let this keep us down. There was more of a determined sense of urgency to keep moving."

"You appreciate when things are good," my mother said. "Happiness makes you feel very happy, laughing feels so good, going somewhere and having a good time feels so good, so you become a happy person." In recent years, psychologists have referred to this as post-traumatic growth. My mother paraphrased psychologist John Brantner, who'd once compared grief and suffering to a metal spring. Grief and suffering compress the spring down, she said, "but when you experience happiness, it springs up" even higher. Over her desk, she hung a big yellow button. "Enjoy life," it reads. "This is not a dress rehearsal."

The more I learned of Jon's story, the more the story began to come to life in new and surprising ways. I began to see connections in things I had never seen or thought about before, sometimes in ways that unsettled me. For years, I had walked past the banners in our synagogue in Tampa, the ones depicting the prophesy of the Child Shall Lead Them, and the story of Jonathan and David. In all this time, however, I had never read the story of Jonathan and David, and, one afternoon, I looked up the translation. I read of the two friends' love for each other, and how Jonathan's father, King Saul of Israel, had grown jealous of David after David had killed Goliath and married his daughter.

But what really struck me was what happened next. Saul decides to have David killed, and Jonathan devises a plan to save his friend. He tells David to hide in the woods. Jonathan would then come to the woods with a bow and arrow, and shoot arrows into the woods in a certain direction if the coast was clear. Jonathan does this, and David returns from the woods to find that he's safe. But the two must say good-bye, and, when they do, the story says, "They cried together, but David cried the most."

Woods. Bows. Arrows. Jonathan. David. David crying the most. It was strange. I was never religious, and I took the Bible stories as just stories from which one could glean whatever one liked. My brain blended the story with my own, twisting the two. Jonathan went into the woods. The killers came with their bows and arrows. Jonathan died, and I, David, cried for him.

I didn't know what, if anything, it meant, but the parallels felt striking. Such strange connections happened again, like when I listened to the only tape I had of Jon's voice, and heard that it was him describing the murder of Underdog by Simon Bar Sinister. There was more too, like the fact that my daughter, who had been named for him, would later have a bat mitzvah that randomly fell on the same weekend as the anniversary of Jon's death.

But most powerful was when my mother called to tell me she'd been moving a file cabinet in my father's home office when she found something amazing underneath: letters and poems of Jon's. I couldn't believe it. She had no recollection of these papers, and neither did Andy or I. The few treasured possessions we had of Jon's had been in the same small wooden box for decades. If my father had found these papers, he would have shared them with us. The only explanation—the only rational one—was that we had all somehow forgotten these existed, and that seemed absurd. But no matter: the fact that my mother found them, after decades, just weeks before I finished writing this memoir, was incredible enough.

Soon after, I received a manila envelope from my mom with Jon's papers inside. I had never seen anything he'd written, never heard his voice other than that one audiotape, and felt almost as though I couldn't even focus on the first page I pulled out. It was a one-paragraph story from December 1971, about two years before his death, when he was nine, written in blocky pencil on lined paper. "Trees and Birds," it is titled. "One day there was a beautiful tree in the garden. What a garden. But did you know that some children use to play there but now there dead and then some children moved in the house. The End."

I felt light-headed as I lowered the papers in my hands. A beautiful tree in the garden. Children played there. Now they're dead? I read the page again for clues. What was this? There was a red star in the upper right-hand corner. It must have been a school assignment of some sort. Maybe he was paraphrasing something he had read. Maybe he had just watched some filmstrip he had to describe. Or, who knows, maybe it was his own invention. My mind reeled. Was it a premonition of his own death in the woods? The "garden" across from our street? The woods, in fact, where homes had since been built and, as he wrote, "some children moved in."

It didn't make sense. But nothing about his death ever did. I turned the page. "The Ugly Goblin," this one was titled from an unmarked year. "There was a ugly, ugly, ugly, ugly, ugly, ugly, spooky, spooky, ugly, yucky goblin. He was very, very ugly. But there was a friendly ghost named Gus and he lived with his best friend and he was a goblin but he was not that ugly. And did you know that there was a bat his name was fatso? And he was so fat, fat, fat, fat, fat, fat, fat, fat, fat, fat. Boy—he was so fat he popped! All he's [bones] fell out. And he was very stupid because he had no brain and he did not know anything at all. The goblin was the stupid one. The End."

Again my mind clawed for clues, reading the words like a cipher. A ghost? More death. The bat, another sign. The bat was stupid, the goblin too. Perhaps this was Jon's way of saying that he felt stupid, that he was struggling with his learning problems. I stopped myself in midthought. What was I doing now? What was I trying to divine? I flipped the page to find a short letter, written the summer before he died, when he was at overnight camp, the same camp where I had seen him posing shirtless and flipping a bird. "Dear Mom Dad Andy and also David," he wrote. My name, David. So strange to see it in his own hand; this the only time I'd ever seen him use it at all. "I'm still having a great time," he went on, "tell David thanks for he's nice letters he's ever had. How's Andy Mom and Dad and David. I hope there OK. Love, Jon."

I read it again, savoring his mention of my name, not just once but three times. My name, David, his little brother, my big brother Jon. And I couldn't help but find more meaning in his words. This was it, the only reference to me at all, and what was he doing? He was thanking me for writing. Was I overreaching by thinking this? Was I seeking his approval? Or was I simply tuning in to some otherworldly missive, some message he sent to me—astonishingly—in the final days of my writing my book about him? I didn't know what to make of it and felt a bit foolish trying to make anything of it at all. I consulted my rabbi for insight, and he said the same thing that a religious friend of mine had told me: perhaps this is Jon here with you while you're writing your book.

But Jon would come to me in one more way. It happened on a clear, blue day in January 2013, and I was sitting at my desk at home, leafing through the eight-hundred-page case file while working on my book. I thought I had read everything, but there was apparently one thing I missed. In the middle of the case file, I came to an eight-page summary by the police of the first two days after Jon went missing. It started with the missing-person call from my dad. "Very briefly," I read, "the child's parents reported that their eleven-year-old son Jonathan Kushner, had just finished cutting the lawn and his five-year-old brother asked him to go to the 7-Eleven store to get him some candy."

As I read the words, I reached up to turn off the music on my computer. Then I read the end of the line again, focusing on the words "brother asked him to go to the 7-Eleven store to get him some candy." They had my age wrong—I was four—but that was not what hit me. It was the rest of it, the part about how I had asked Jon to go get candy for me. He went because I asked him? He went for this reason alone?

Throughout my life, I had gone through so many iterations of my final exchange with him, and, yes, I did recall standing on the sidewalk asking him for the alligator candy. But I never entertained the thought that the *reason* he went to the store at all was because I had asked him. I thought he was just going anyway, and I had asked him to get me something while he was there. That thought alone had given me sometimes unbearable guilt growing up, and now, forty years later, out of the blue, the guilt came walloping back.

He had gone for me? Because I asked him? My mind and heart raced. Intellectually, I knew well enough that I should not assume guilt for his murder, that I alone was not responsible for his death. I knew that the living play self-destructive games of what-if when someone dies. Friends of Jon's had been asking themselves, *What if we had played with him that morning, and he hadn't gone?* Teachers at IDS had asked themselves, *What if we had allowed other students to go down that path when the killers were there?*

But as much as I knew it was just my mind corroding me, I couldn't fight it. I felt responsible. I felt awful. Even though this was on the page in black and white, I still didn't know if it was completely true. But why would my father tell the police that Jon had gone to get candy for me? I thought back to the day when I was sixteen, and I sat with him on the back porch, listening to the news of Witt's execution on the transistor radio, and how my dad told me, for the first time, the details of Jon's murder. I remembered how, when I brought up my memory of my last conversation with Jon, my dad corrected me, telling me that, no, I wasn't the last to see him. The memory hadn't happened. The last person to see Jon was him.

I'd since wondered if perhaps my dad was protecting me—if he was purposefully revising the story so that I wouldn't beat myself up for having dispatched Jon to his death. As much as I thought that would be out of character for my father, since he was always so direct with me when we discussed such matters, now, with him dead, I would have no way of knowing. I called my mother to ask her what she thought: Could Dad have been lying to me? She agreed that that wasn't something he would do; he was not one to mask the truth. My mother's memory of what happened to the candy was hazy, but when I told her about the police report, she thought it wasn't accurate. As far as she recalled, Jon was going to the store anyway, and I had simply asked him to get me something while he was there.

Still, the truth felt like it was eluding me, and my emotions of guilt were already unleashed. I wasn't trying to be a martyr, I was just trying to cope. But I couldn't write anymore. I couldn't read. I had to get up and walk outside, breathe the crisp winter air. Guilt was corrosive, an acid, numbing me to the world around me, casting me back into the body of myself forty years before. I replayed the conversation with Jon again, calling it up like a hologram before my eyes. I heard myself talking with him about the alligator candy, saw him shifting his feet on the pedals, and I wanted to scream out, "No, don't go! I don't need the candy. Don't get it. Don't get it for me. Stay home. Stay here. I know what awaits you. I can see through the woods. I see the men there parked in their car with their Cracker Jack and Coke. I know what awaits you. I know everything!"

But I couldn't scream out. I couldn't travel through time. It was written. The story was done. Jon went to the store and never came back. And I would have to live with that, live with the missing pieces of his story that remained despite everything I had learned. But at least I knew enough to understand that even if I were responsible for Jon's decision to go to the store that day, I did not put Witt and Tillman there. I did not set the crime into motion. And perhaps Jon would have gone anyway. His death was beyond his or my control.

As I sit here at my desk writing these words, I have become filled with a sense that my brother is here with me. The peace sign that used to hang in his room hangs on my wall. My desk is covered with his case file. There's a picture of him in a small white frame beside me. I have never been one to believe in life after death or that people communicate with us after they die. I believe, though, that perhaps their energy remains in some form; something we can access in ways we can't fully understand.

All I know is that right here, right now, after so many months of reading and writing about Jon, I feel his presence like never before. The alligator candy is no longer just a reminder of evil and loss, of guilt and pain, it's a symbol of my connection to my brother and the gift he had gone to get for me. And a part of me hears him now in my head:

"David," he says, "it's not your fault. Don't do this to yourself. David, I love you."

And I know that this book is, perhaps more than anything, my way of telling him I love him too.

44

MY DAUGHTER learned to ride her bike on the same sidewalk where I last saw Jon. As she eagerly climbed up on her seat, I put my hands on her shoulders and began to push, breaking into a stride as she pedaled. Then came that inevitable moment: when her wheels went faster than I could run, and her shoulders left my palms, and she kept going, moving her feet, steering delightedly on her own as I watched her go, and then return.

In the years since, I've been able to find inspiration in the person who came to represent that freedom to me most of all: Jon. I can finally do something that I could never fully do before: imagine him alive. I know that while his death was so tragic, he was never more alive than his very last ride. He was a boy on a bike, alone and independent, racing through the woods with candy in his basket for him and me. The wind was in his face. He was pedaling fast. He was heading home. And he was free.

ACKNOWLEDGMENTS

SPECIAL THANKS TO Jofie Ferrari-Adler, Jonathan Karp, Alessandra Bastagli, David McCormick, Mary Ann Naples, and everyone at Simon & Schuster for making this book possible. Thank you to my friends and family for their love and support. I'm deeply grateful to all those who shared their memories with me for this book and helped my family through our most difficult time.

ABOUT THE AUTHOR

DAVID KUSHNER is the author of *Masters of Doom: How Two Guys Created an Empire and Transformed Pop Culture; Jonny Magic and the Card Shark Kids: How a Gang of Geeks Beat the Odds and Stormed Las Vegas; Levittown: Two Families, One Tycoon, and the Fight for Civil Rights in America's Legendary Suburb; Jacked: The Outlaw Story of Grand Theft Auto; The Bones of Marianna: A Reform School, a Terrible Secret, and a Hundred-Year Fight for Justice; Prepare to Meet Thy Doom: And More True Gaming Stories;* and *The World's Most Dangerous Geek: And Other True Hacking Stories.*

A Ferris professor of journalism at Princeton University, Kushner has written for publications including *The New Yorker, Vanity Fair, GQ, The New York Times Magazine*, and *Rolling Stone*, where he is a contributing editor. The winner of the New York Press Club award for Best Feature Reporting, Kushner is featured in *The Best American Crime Reporting*, and *The Columbia Journalism Review's Best Business Writing* anthologies. *The Bones of Marianna* was chosen by Amazon as a Best Digital Single of 2013.